Praise for *Fake Work*

"*Fake Work* gets to the heart of what organizations are about, conducting work activities that create real value as defined by an organization's strategies. It is amazing that despite all the efforts and programs pulled together to improve how organizations operate, leaders and consultants in their exuberance often overlook the most important factor, the work itself. Brent and Gaylan provide a clear and easy-to-read text that illustrates experiences we can all relate to. More important, they provide a road map for how to get out of this conundrum."

—Curt J. Howes, president, OP Strategies

"*Fake Work* provides a different view of how to get people having an impact on their organizational goals and results. Using many simple but painfully true and recognizable stories, the book unravels the numerous issues organizations face around having extremely busy and hardworking employees who may not, in many cases, be impacting the bottom line. The good news is Peterson and Nielson lay out deceptively simple but effective steps to resolve this. If you are prepared to get to the root of ensuring everyone is contributing to results, then this is the way to go!"

Stephen Krempl, president,
Krempl Communications International

"I have worked for more than fifty years in the business world, from senior positions in multinational corporations to a wide variety of entrepreneurial ventures, and this seminal work is the first time I have ever seen or even heard of any serious examination of the disconnect between effort expended and work (results) accomplished.

"Following the techniques outlined in the book should appeal to everyone in all kinds of workplaces, whether the home, charitable organizations, or bread-and-butter enterprises. Doing so will align the person's real work with the organization's objectives and goals. At that point, the individual's contribution to the bottom line will be visible, and he or she will enjoy a substantial boost in self-worth and the satisfaction of making a real difference.

"Everyone from the entry-level person through middle man-

agement to top management will find this book useful in guiding them to make their work real work, not fake work."
—LeRoy K. Speirs, National Advisory Council of the Marriott School of Management, Brigham Young University

"As I read *Fake Work* I became increasingly aware that I was awash in these issues, the mastery of which is required of all successful businesspeople. These were the issues of effectiveness with which Peterson organized and imbued the Center for Entrepreneurship at the Marriott School of Management, as its first director. *Fake Work* is an intriguing insight into execution issues."
—Nyal D. McMullin, Saratoga, California

"This book poses interesting questions that challenge commonly used practices in the workplace and takes you through a journey to realize new heights of efficiencies. The concept cuts through culture and is truly an eye-opener."
—Mohamed Farouk Hafeez, chief executive human resources officer, Americana Group S.A.E., Cairo, Egypt

"*Fake Work* is an excellent way to describe what I have seen in many organizations during my more than thirty years of management consulting work. *Fake Work* describes situations that are common on both sides of the Atlantic Ocean. I am convinced that you as a reader of this book will be motivated to find ways to stop doing fake work and start doing real work."
—Håkan Palm, CEO and founder, HåBe Konsultation AB, Stockholm, Sweden

"*Fake Work* delivers practical and well-proven techniques to identify gaps and fill them with *real* work. Brent and Gaylan have worked with several multinational companies in Singapore from entertainment to research to manufacturing firms; and all of them have found the principles of fake work to be extremely useful and are still using these principles to track real work! Master the skills of real work at work and at home, and you will have lots of time to play!"

—Tan Bee Wan, Ph.D., chief executive officer,
Integrative Learning Corporation Ltd., Singapore

"Are you tired, unchallenged, unfocused, and having no fun in your work? If you are, you are probably suffering from an overdose of fake work. Get this book and learn how to get rid of fake work—it will restore you to a life of energy and purpose. You owe it to yourself, your company, and your family to get rid of fake work once and for all."

—A. C. Ho, executive consultant,
Right Management, Singapore

"When I look around any organization, everyone is very busy, working very hard and staying very late to get work done. When I look at results, somehow there is a mismatch between all the work being done and the results attained. The simplicity of the concepts and applications in *Fake Work* will help any organization move from fake work to real work, thereby having all of their resources aligned to achieving the same goals. If you are looking for something that is practical and not just hype, take the time to read and apply these concepts."

—Darryl Wee, chief commercial officer,
Nestronics Ltd., Singapore

"*Fake Work* is a culmination of a wealth of research and experience that have been utilized in identifying and addressing a problem currently endemic to global management: work not aligned with organizational strategies. *Fake Work* is an apt title for an ingenious concept. Brent Peterson and Gaylan Nielson have developed an approach that is at once practical, simple and efficient to eliminate fake work and the problems associated with it. This book is a must-have for any organization."

—Tamer M. Badrawi, executive director,
Future Generation Foundation, Cairo, Egypt

FAKE
WORK

Why People Are Working Harder
Than Ever but Accomplishing Less,
and How to Fix the Problem

BRENT D.
PETERSON *and* GAYLAN W.
NIELSON

Simon Spotlight Entertainment

New York   London   Toronto   Sydney

Simon Spotlight Entertainment
A Division of Simon & Schuster, Inc.
1230 Avenue of the Americas
New York, NY 10020

First Simon Spotlight Entertainment hardcover edition January 2009

SIMON SPOTLIGHT ENTERTAINMENT and colophon
are trademarks of Simon & Schuster, Inc.

For information about special discounts for bulk purchases,
please contact Simon & Schuster Special Sales at 1-800-456-6798
or business@simonandschuster.com

Designed by Nancy Singer

Manufactured in the United States of America

10 9 8 7 6 5 4 3 2 1

Library of Congress Cataloging-in-Publication Data
Peterson, Brent D.
    Fake work: why people are working harder than ever but accomplishing less, and
how to fix the problem / Brent D. Peterson and Gaylan W. Nielson.—1st ed.
        p.   cm.
    Includes bibliographical references and index.
    1. Organizational effectiveness.   2. Work.   I. Nielson, Gaylan W.   II. Title.
    HD58.9.P48   2008
    331.25'6—dc22   2008037584

ISBN-13: 978-1-4169-4824-7
ISBN-10:   1-4169-4824-4

I dedicate this book to four teachers and friends who have influenced my life and who helped me become who I am: Charles Metten for forcing me to be Uncle Sid, Gary Peterson for convincing me I was capable of more than I thought, Carl Weaver for sticking with me and encouraging me, and R. Wayne Pace, who saw something of worth in me and encouraged me to do real work and avoid fake work.

—Brent D. Peterson

I dedicate this book to Elaine, to my wonderful children and grandchildren, and to my parents. But they all know that Elaine is our magnetic north, our sacred center, our coach and guide. She is my best friend, my travel companion, and the kind of supporter and ally that a man could only have dreamed up.

—Gaylan W. Nielson

CONTENTS

FOREWORD
by Stephen R. Covey

THIS IS AN amazing book. And so needed today!

Just consider this story: You're flying to a business meeting in Chicago. You land on time, go to the car rental place, and rent a car. The person at the desk gives you a map. You find your rental car in the lot and drive off, happily on your way. The problem is, the person at the desk made a mistake and handed you a map of Philadelphia. That was the only source of information that you had. You're totally lost and utterly confused, so you call your business associate, who is waiting for you at the meeting, and tell him that you can hardly find your way out of the airport. He glibly tells you to try harder, so you double your speed, but now you're getting increasingly lost twice as fast. You call your associate again in a state of utter discouragement, complaining that you can find no landmark that resembles anything on the map. He senses your negative energy and tells you to think positively. He even gives one of his favorite little speeches about the importance of PMA—Positive Mental Attitude—and sings a few lines of "Your altitude is governed by your attitude" to you. So you start thinking positively and now you don't care that you're lost. You're happy and contented in your lost state. You never really wanted to attend the meeting, anyway.

But the problem had nothing to do with your behavior or with your attitude. It had everything to do with a bad map.

That's what this book is about. It gives us the right map about work. Now of course, if you have the correct map, then behavior and attitude become important. But until you have a correct map, to change your behavior or to shape up your attitude would be worthless. In almost every field of endeavor, significant breakthroughs are break *withs:* breaks with old ways of thinking, old mental models, in short—bad maps.

Take a moment and consider the following question: What is more central to life than work? Work is the major activity that occupies most of our time every day. Therefore, it is supremely important to get a correct map, or a correct view, of what real work is.

That's why this book is so valuable, particularly today, when we have moved from the Industrial Age into the Knowledge Worker Age. In the Industrial Age, over 80 percent of the value added to goods and services came from machinery and manual labor, and there was a greater alignment and connection between this kind of work and producing desired results. But in the Knowledge Worker Age, 70 to 80 percent of the value added to goods and services comes from knowledge work—that is, human input, where the connection between such work and desired results has become blurred. In this global, digitized economy, competition is ten times what it was before, and the necessity to avoid fake work and do real work will make all the difference, producing success or failure.

Another reason it's so important to get a correct map of work is that organizations are currently under tremendous pressure to produce more for less, and yet employees are, for the most part, disempowered or even disallowed from using their capabilities, their intelligence, their talents, and their passion. What a dilemma—pressure to produce more for less yet prevented from using talent! Fake work is deeply demoralizing and disempowering and contributes to the metastasizing emotional cancers of interpersonal conflict, interdepartmental rivalries, hidden agendas, complaining, criticizing, angry contention, and profound cynicism. And people often feel that they're being victimized by the system or a bad boss or some other corporate bad guy.

Employees today are caught in the activity trap—they're busy to the hilt but profoundly misaligned with well-thought-through strategies and desired results. In fact, in most cases, even if the strategies are well thought through, they're not understood down the line. Or if the strategies are understood, most people don't know how their role connects to those strategic goals. Then the whole world of work revolves around execution gaps. The activity trap becomes institutionalized and enculturated, and eventually many come to assume that this is simply the way things are—they start to accept that most reports are never even looked at, most meetings don't need to be held, and little by little they become codependent and complicit in maintaining this terribly costly fake reality. Then more and more people complain, criticize, and blame, blame, blame. (This is sometimes called a self-fulfilling prophecy, where you produce the evidence to support your perception.)

I encourage you to seriously study this book; it is so beautifully, sequentially organized into two parts: Part 1, Understanding Fake Work and Its Causes; and Part 2, The Pathways out of Fake Work, and the stories wonderfully represent and illustrate each of the points made in this sequence. If you allow the sequence to have its way with you, as I did, you will have a growing conviction of the difference between fake work and real work. You will also feel excited and energized about fixing the problem.

This fixing process is immensely practical and hands-on, but also fundamentally principle-based, so that you can adapt these principles to most every situation. I've had years of involvement in both doing fake work and researching fake work, and I've learned from personal experience the sense of satisfaction and fulfillment that comes from doing real work that is aligned with carefully thought through strategic results. The combination of the paradigm of fake and real work and the stories in this book will give you the confidence to resolve and deal with the execution gaps that are so pervasive in most organizations.

Synergy means the whole is greater than the sum of the parts. These two authors have produced a superior, synergistic product on a subject of immense importance. Gaylan Nielson was a senior leader at FranklinCovey at a period when I traveled extensively, so I don't know him well, but I know of his accomplishments and his work with our consulting group—helping us forge new services and building long-term relationships with our clients with a whole new perspective. That new perspective manifests itself as a fresh angle, a unique, creative contribution to this book and to his work with Brent Peterson in building several companies that have grown into The Work Itself Group. I have known Brent Peterson for many years and believe him to be one of the finest educators I have ever known. The textbooks he has written have been brilliant and well accepted. We have worked together as professors at a university and then as consultants, trainers, researchers, and writers in a marvelous training company. He has served as a real work leader, CEO, entrepreneur, and business owner and developer for many years. There is true synergy in this wonderful book, which I commend to you as being foundational in helping organizations to align and to execute on that which they have strategically decided to be worthy to focus on. This book should be read by leaders, by managers, by trainers and by workers.

I wish you all the best in your study of this new mindset, and acquisition of the new tool set and skill set that enables the movement from the activity trap to both institutionalizing and enculturating real work.

INTRODUCTION
Why Do You Need a Book About Fake Work?

THIS BOOK IS about work—specifically, how to do work that is effective and that leads individuals and organizations to achieve results. Fake work is work that is not targeting or aligned with the strategies and goals of the company. That may seem simple, but we have discovered that at all too many workplaces much of the work that people do *doesn't* achieve results. It's because workplaces are plagued by what we call "fake work"—simply put, work that wastes time and resources, work that drains companies of both dollars and morale.

As consultants for more than twenty years, we have researched the way people conduct work, and the various approaches to work, from the scientific movement through the human-relations movement to the present. While we are products of the human-relations movement, we are making a decisive shift to find the sweet spot between the scientific and the humanistic approach: We care about the people, but the focus on *the right work* must be recalculated in the equation.

During those years we watched, conducted, and participated in many training and development programs that were meant to make organizations stronger and more productive. And we came to a disturbing conclusion: While development programs, with their emphasis on human interaction, do help people, they tend to contribute little toward the real goals of the organization. Of course, companies and other organizations must treat their people well, but the real question needs to be: *What can we do to increase our performance?*

The answer: *View work with an eye toward results*. When individuals, teams, and organizations focus on the work they do, productivity miracles begin to happen. As we began to do our research, with a focus on work, we made an important discovery—much of the hard work people do for their organization does little to link people to the strategies that are intended to help the organization achieve its goals. In fact, our research shows that across all the organizations we have studied, about half the work that people do fails to advance the organizations' strategies.

We call this ineffective work "fake work." It might seem important and it is often time-consuming and difficult to complete, but it is *not* strategically important. We realized that if we could help an organization enable its workers to do more *real work*—work that is aligned to strategy—then the organization would better execute critical tasks and achieve stronger results.

Our Research and Experience Taught Us to Focus on Work

This book is the culmination of many years of research and a wide range of experience. We have worked with companies large and small, government agencies, nonprofits, schools, and community groups. And in every case, fake work keeps cropping up as a serious foe of productivity and organizational results. We have worked with organizations to develop and implement strategies, to align teams and individuals with those strategies, and to help individuals perform critical tasks regarding the strategies. We have done measurement studies to analyze the true impact of this work on organizational results. To put it simply, we've done our homework—and we're happy to share our answers with you.

This Book Is for People at Work

We wrote this book for everyone who works—in businesses, government agencies, community groups, even families. And we didn't focus on a specific audience, such as leaders or managers, because the chain of responsibility for work includes everyone at every level. Though we usually refer to "companies" in this book, we are addressing all organizations where good people are trying to do good work and get valuable results. We know that almost all of those organizations are trying to deliver products and services that serve customers and the broader society.

We have worked at all levels with and for organizations, and we have extraordinary empathy and respect for the enormous commitment and desire to do great things by so many people. And that's why it's so painful to see fake work prevent these committed people and organizations from serving their customers as well as they could.

A Story Book

As we've lived, observed, and explained the concept of fake work over the past few years, we have collected stories and been inundated with accounts from people who have been bedeviled by fake work at their own jobs. In writing this book, we decided we could best illustrate our points by including a number of their stories. While the accounts vary in many ways, they all illustrate the burden—and the danger—of fake work.

As we share them here, we have used fictional names and changed identifying details of the people and organizations. The stories are used to illustrate the painful failings of individuals and teams. But failures often give direction for future successes, and we hope the anonymous accounts we present here will help you root out the fake work in your own organization.

Our Journeys: Common Roots, Diverse Paths

We both come from rural backgrounds and grew up with a very strong sense of work and its direct link to how people survive. If someone didn't raise and bale hay, the cows didn't eat, and they didn't give milk.

Brent, a professor, has worked with organizations for the past thirty years trying to help them be more successful. For the past ten years he has been on a crusade to teach organizations about strategy, alignment, and execution. He has also owned several successful consulting businesses.

Gaylan, a writer and playwright, backed into the business world—an ignorant and uncomfortable visitor—who saw himself as an outsider. But over time, that very quality became an important aspect of his consulting and his point of view. He has built several companies that have grown into the Work Itself Group, developed with Brent, and has served in many leadership positions.

We hope you enjoy this book—and that it helps you eliminate fake work and move toward real, productive work.

PART 1

Understanding Fake Work and Its Causes

CHAPTER 1

Fake Work: Building a Road to Nowhere

Joyful is the accumulation of good work.

— *Buddha*

SUPPOSE YOU ARE building a road on a mountainside leading to the site for your new cabin. You have worked for months clearing sagebrush and aspen trees. You've moved rocks and filled in road bed through the exhausting heat, the raging downpours, even early snow. You've pushed forward, working from your best understanding of the surveyor's plans. Your road winds over a dusty hill, cuts through the trees, moves along a rocky ridge, and then—you find yourself looking down from the edge of a cliff.

Fake work looks and feels like that. The building of the road was purposeful. Your effort was admirable. The blood, sweat, and tears you poured into the project were real and your commitment was profound. *But none of that really matters!* You are still left with a road to nowhere.

So many of us have dedicated weekends and long nights to a project, proposal, or presentation that ended up being canceled, ignored, or dismissed—essentially roads to nowhere—and see all one's efforts lead to nothing. That is the road to fake work—work that, at the end of long days, weeks, months, or even years, just seems to drop off a cliff.

What Is Real Work and What Is Fake Work?

We spend more than half our lives and a vast percentage of our waking hours going to work, being at work, leaving work, and thinking about work—even when we're not *at* work. What we sometimes miss, when we think about work, is outcomes.

Real work, as we define it, is work that is critical and aligned to the key goals and strategies of an organization—any organization, corporation, nonprofit company, government agency, church, school, or family. It is work that is essential for the organization's short-term and long-term survival.

Fake work, on the other hand, is effort under the *illusion* of value. Fake work is work that is not targeting or aligned with the strategies and goals of the company. Fake work is what happens when people lose sight of their personal or company goals— whether it's increasing sales, opening new offices, or designing new products—and what, amid all the work being done, they're *actually doing* to achieve those goals. Prime examples of fake work—which drains both the individual and the company—are meaningless paperwork, time-wasting meetings, empty training initiatives, or countless other activities that do nothing to move us toward our objectives, either as individuals or as companies.

Often it is easy to identify fake work, simply because it is so blatantly obvious and stupid. One manager, Ricky, describes one such situation:

PICKED TO WASTE MY TIME

I was put on a committee to study my company's travel policy. A lot of complaints had surfaced, and employees seemed to have a lot of problems interpreting the policy correctly. But most of us on this committee felt that the real intent of upper management, which put together the committee, was only to validate the current policy, because we had been through the same kind of charade before with other issues.

In the first meeting, Katrina, a committee member, asked,

"Does anyone think that we can make any changes, or make any difference at all?" Most of us answered no. Kurt, another coworker, added, "Nothing is going to change, so let's write up a proposal and get this over with."

I had been here before. I'm in HR, and last year I was asked to renew our benefits plan and make recommendations on changes. So I wrote up a long analysis and proposed a lot of changes. Then later I learned from a coworker that most of those changes had already been determined. They just wanted to say that they'd asked for my contribution. I knew—most of us knew—that we could write or propose anything, and the leaders would say they had given all the issues due attention and were confident that the current policy was working.

There were a few committee members who felt honored to have a seat at the table. But not me, not most. I just wondered why management would pick me—"honor me"—with a total waste of my time.

But we went ahead and did our work. We reviewed the travel policy and benchmarked it against other company policies. We gathered data and recommended four key changes in the policy that seemed to respond to the criticisms. We filed a report and we presented our recommendations to some key people.

And what do you think happened? Sure enough, a while later, the company leaders announced that, after looking at all the data and reviewing our report, they would make "no changes at this time." We can't say we were at all surprised, but we sure were annoyed.

Other times, fake work can be hard, dreadfully hard, to detect, as we will explore in the following chapters. As the next story illustrates, the line between real work and fake work can be thin, but very costly and time-consuming.

ENGINEERING VS. REPORTING

A large engineering firm asked us to pinpoint areas where its engineers and managers could be more productive. Management thought the fault lay with engineers who were not planning and organizing their work effectively. But we discovered a more obvious culprit that was stealing enormous amounts of essential, client-focused work time each week: the lengthy activity reports that the engineers had to write and file.

Management expected a thorough activity report from each engineer each week. In addition, the engineers were also to file monthly reports. The reports were extensive, averaging about fifteen pages each. In fact, the reports took about *four days per month per engineer* to prepare. Managers told us the reports were important. We didn't disagree, but we were concerned. For one thing, we found that most of the content in the weekly and monthly reports was lengthy narrative that was already captured in their daily logs.

We asked several managers if they would show us how they used the engineers' reports and what important information they disclosed. One manager, Rafael, seemed to represent the other managers well. He pulled a huge stack of reports from his in-box, complaining that he would never get through them. We asked Rafael to mark, with a yellow highlighter, the parts of the reports he was interested in reading—what was most important. He stopped reading and started hunting for the pertinent information by jumping from the front of the report to the back and then skimmed it over page by page. When we asked what he did with the reports when he was finished, he showed us a huge bookshelf crammed floor to ceiling with past reports.

We then asked him why he read the last page so early. He said, "If anything of value appears in the report, I usually find it in the last few pages." Then we tried to pinpoint what he was looking for. We reviewed the highlighted content and found that Rafael was looking for three key pieces of information:

1. Problems that had to be solved
2. Recommendations that managers or others needed to act on to solve the problems
3. Conclusions from projects. Something final of importance.

Given that most of the managers had needs quite similar to Rafael's, we helped the company design a two-page summary that the engineers could file every week, instead of the fifteen-page reports they were currently writing. It had three headings:

1. Problems found on _____ project
2. Recommendations for action
3. Conclusions regarding _____ project

Then we cut out the monthly report entirely because the short summaries gave the managers all the information they needed.

This simple change significantly reduced the time managers spent reviewing the reports. But it was the engineers who saved the most time; their reporting time was reduced by 75 percent, freeing three more days each month for them to do real work. More important, eliminating so many hours of wasteful, fake work on the part of both management and the engineers, added to their enjoyment of the work, helped solve retention issues, and improved overall job satisfaction.

As challenging as it sometimes is to answer, can you afford *not* to ask yourself the critical question: Am I doing fake work? And once you've asked yourself if you've fallen into the fake-work trap, other important questions will arise: Are my coworkers doing fake work? Where does fake work begin, and who has the ability to control it? How do leaders affect fake work? How can work teams control the value of their work? What about individuals? Throughout this book, we hope to illuminate these questions and offer meaningful answers. In the process, we will challenge readers to ask the right questions, to understand the issues, and to find their way back from the road to nowhere.

The Changing Nature of Work

Go to a bar, restaurant, hotel, or sporting event on any given night, and you'll find people checking their work voice mail and reading work-related e-mail on their BlackBerrys or iPhones; you'll see conference calls happening on commuter trains at 6 a.m.; and in the airport you'll see people who routinely travel to a faraway city during the day for work and return home at ten p.m., often multiple nights a week. As a culture, we're defined by our work, and many of us are consumed by doing our jobs all the time. We're working harder and faster than ever before, and we're doing it on a 24/7 schedule.

But our research points up a painful fact: All too often the incredibly hard work spent on a project or task is not what needs to be done to meet company goals: It is fake work. The intent is to accomplish good work. The intent is to be responsible. The intent is to be proud of our work. But can you be working hard, with good intentions, with amazing effort, and still be doing fake work? Sadly, yes, and way too often. Much of the reason for this grim reality is found in the fact that work has changed. In fact, the very nature of how we see and measure work has shifted dramatically in a very short time, and we must ensure that we understand real work and fake work in the context of these changes. Plenty has been written about the shift from products to services, from manufacturing to knowledge and information workers, from low use of technology to high use. And each of these shifts makes a huge difference in how we perceive work.

The following is a story shared by Collin, the CEO of a technology consulting firm, in which he takes a mental journey as he walks through his work environment and queries the activities he's observing.

WHAT IS THIS THING CALLED WORK?

I am walking around our office building and people are busy—very busy. There is a lot of quiet space, and a lot of people are talking on cell phones—possibly to our customers or colleagues around the world. There are lots of people frantically typing on computers. I feel like peeking through the shades of offices and over the cubicle walls to see what is actually happening on those computer screens and eavesdropping on all those cell phone calls. I know we are billing for work, but I don't know how much is justified—I mean, how much of what we are billing for is real work? How efficient are we? Sometimes I don't know if work is happening at all. I know I employ good people who are highly involved and very busy. But I don't know enough about our focus. I don't know how much of the activity I see is just distraction.

I hear Janice laugh in the distance. Some people talk over their cubicle walls. The concept of work is not the same at all as when I was young. Information is a nebulous concept. Because we get paid for thinking, I am careful not to interrupt, but I am concerned that people don't know what is truly valuable and critical in our work. I am not sure I have helped make it clear. I am not sure I always know what is valuable and critical myself.

Vincent is at his computer. He answers e-mails, writes e-mails, develops ideas, shares them with his colleague working in Malaysia. He researches the Web. Is it what he—and we—need to be doing? Jared brings me two hundred pages of articles on design that he has reviewed. I didn't want to discourage him, but there was nothing in those pages that addressed our big issues or served our clients. I don't know how at-risk we are because I can't possibly know enough about all this amorphous work and how clients perceive the value. A lot of this activity feels like work. People stay late and come in early. Weekends are not much quieter here, and even then the e-mails keep flowing to me and everyone else. And yet I see work tasks tackled on the weekends evaporating into meaningless discussions. I am guessing that I could change some lives if we could define "critical" and eliminate as much else as possible.

Collin's ponderings explore the changing nature of work and point to the fact that it is sometimes hard to know if work is being done at all—because banging on the computer or searching the Web has as much potential to be fake work as real. The shift challenges the way we think about and how we see, understand, and measure the effectiveness and relevance of work. Activity alone does not define work's value. In a manufacturing environment, drilling holes and placing bolts through the holes defines the work, making work and intent easy to connect. Baling hay in a field is easy to see as real work; farmhands are either baling or they're not.

Collin won't be able to see whether his company is on track unless he acquires a better understanding of the actual work his employees need to be doing and unless he improves his evaluation skills. Collin is wondering if he has done his job—defining and clarifying the critical elements of his employees' work. He also wonders if he even knows what those elements are. So if he doubts himself, he has a right to wonder whether others in his company are doing what they need to be doing.

As companies employ more and more remote workers, people working at staggered hours, and people working on research and less product-related work, our view of work must be adjusted. The models for effective management, the measures of success, and our ideas about value have been turned on their heads. The result is that many of us still make the mistake of equating time spent with being truly useful to the company. We routinely run into employees who think they need to be the last one out of the office every night or who try to get involved in every project so that they become "indispensable." But does that make these people great workers? No. An MIT study suggests that workers put in far more hours at work than is necessary.

Productivity is difficult to measure, and official statistics measure it merely as the Gross Domestic Product adjusted for inflation divided by the total number of hours worked. But if this measure means anything at all, an average worker today needs to work a mere 11 hours per week to produce as much as one working 40 hours per week in 1950. (The data here is from the U.S., but productivity increases in Europe and Japan have been of the same magnitude.) The conclusion is inescapable: a worker should be able to earn the same standard of living as a 1950 worker in only 11 hours per week.[1]

While many of us realize that we often spend unnecessary time on tasks and projects, it raises a critical question: How many hours do we need to work to accomplish the critical tasks essential to our business? Can we really succeed by working considerably fewer hours than our competitors? A young professional told us the following eye-opening story.

REWARDS FOR THE ILLUSIONS OF WORK

Because we bill for our time, we are rewarded for making twenty-minute tasks into two-hour tasks; we are praised for being up all night, and working long hours means good performance reviews. Our manager said that Carla, my coworker, was really dedicated because she had been online at two in the morning. So I left my instant messenger on all night so it looked like I was online working, and I got praised in our next group meeting. I had been asleep. What the hell! Someone told me that soldiers in Vietnam were told to dig a hole and then fill it in again just so they looked busy during inspections. That's what my job is like sometimes.

1 From U.S. Bureau of Labor Statistics. See http://swiss.csail.mit.edu/~rauch/misc/worktime/

I heard that some business manager said "The 40-hour workweek is dead—welcome to the 60-hour week." Wow. It took them a while to catch up. This isn't a new occurrence; it has been an escalating issue for a couple of decades. I think people are less happy, have less time at home, and participate less at home now that we are expected to be working all the time. People are not working efficiently; they take too much time for everything, and they stretch out their work (especially meetings and conference calls). I think this is all about the need to create the illusion of work. If it looks like work, I can bill for it. If I see you are busy, you are fine. But this isn't real work at all.

We aren't suggesting that all companies suffer from the issues described above. We've observed work that was amazingly efficient and remarkably productive. However, every person, every manager, and every company should ask: How close could we get to an eleven-hour week if we focused just on real, critical work? Then, every company should ask: What additional work should we do that would add value to our company and to our people?

In an ideal workplace, every person would be doing real and valuable work that matters and gets results. Every person would be rewarded for results, not time; and people would prioritize and manage their time to focus on the work of highest value to the company.

Fake Work Is Illusory and Easily Misdiagnosed

Almost everyone has experienced fake work by doing it, seeing it done, and being a victim of it. A common complaint that we hear is that "our company is buried in fake work." That may well be true. But why? Meetings, e-mail, and endless cell phone time seem like easy targets, but they are not necessarily the culprits—not by themselves.

The changing work environment and the new forms of work developed over the last couple of decades make the issue of identifying fake work even more complex, and we want to explore that complexity. Sometimes, *real work and fake work can be exactly the same work*—just under different circumstances. So we can't be dismissive about the subtle and challenging questions required to know the difference.

It's hard to tell whether the time doing research on the Internet is real work or fake work. Determining whether you're making a real contribution to your company can also be difficult when you are:

- Working through the 137 e-mails that came in overnight.
- Giving thoughtful analysis to the endless and mind-numbing spreadsheets Accounting left for review.
- Leaving an endless array of voice mails for coworkers or clients.
- Working on the seventh draft of a proposal.
- Attending yet another critical meeting—at least critical in someone's view.
- Doing a marketing survey and collecting tons of new data.

In the rest of the book, we'll help you find out what may be burying your company in fake work.

Fake Work Is Misunderstood Because It Feels like Work

Many different people in many different roles are in the great chain of fake work. For individuals, fake work is easily mistaken for what you ought to be doing—and what you *want* to be doing—because it generally looks and feels like real and purposeful work. Working hard is not a barometer of fake work, so you may not even see that you are building a road to nowhere. Sometimes you fail to recognize your work as fake. Sometimes you do fake work because you were told to do it. Sometimes fake work is what you're rewarded for doing.

Doing fake work is not necessarily an indication of incompetence, inability, procrastination, or other things that make our work environments ineffective. Fake work occurs when you are not focusing on the work that will move your company forward, and it can show up in many different ways. Some common signs that the road you are building is leading nowhere:

1. You don't really know the strategies of your company and the things that are most important for the whole company to accomplish.
2. You're unable to clearly connect those strategies to what you are doing.
3. You are simply ignorant about the importance of your work.
4. Your hard work is not getting results that matter.
5. You hold meetings without a clear purpose and invite a bunch of people to share in the waste of time.
6. You send e-mails daily to a huge distribution list of coworkers without considering whether they need the information.
7. You hold offsite meetings that provide distraction, not value.
8. You initiate projects that suck up time and are killed for lack of interest.
9. You don't follow through on plans to implement needed changes, or you undermine such plans.
10. You work on a report that you know nobody will read.
11. You assign a report and then ignore it when it's completed.
12. You require paperwork because, well, everybody has to do paperwork.
13. You write proposals that are seen as an important aspect of the selling process, but they don't lead to an increase in sales.
14. You set up a training program that is a lot of fun, is very interesting, and gets great reviews, but the program has no support from management because it doesn't really make a difference to the business.

That is a very short list for a very big problem. Fake work is everywhere. While you may recognize it, it is mired in the complex web of companies, teams, and individuals who don't understand what it is, choose to ignore it, or don't know how to get out of it. It cascades down from managers. It percolates up from teams engaging in fake work that requires attention from others to resolve. Few can escape it. Some are trapped in its claws. It runs the gamut from an annoying nuisance to an insidious and cancerous attack on productivity, effectiveness, and viability.

Fake Work Thrives When We Don't Analyze the Value of Work

So why are people doing work that is clearly fake? Is it because they are stuck in their traditional ways of working? Is it because management needs to keep people busy? Yes! And those are just a few of the neglectful practices that aid fake work.

Fake work thrives where old, outdated processes hang on. It thrives when companies do not clearly articulate the results they need. And it thrives when you and your managers aren't asking whether you are doing fake work.

Companies set expectations, write job descriptions, and review performances that actually promote fake work, which means that you can easily follow directions, complete your assignments, and get promotions—while spending most of your time on fake work. But in the end, people feel the fakeness. Your colleagues know it. You know it, too. You aren't succeeding and neither is your team. The people doing fake work are often at least vaguely aware of the problems that are plaguing the company.

Many Habitual Practices Create Fake Work

The workplace is filled with tradition, precedent, and habit. These are often the harbors of fake work because they institutionalize bad practices. The following account describes employees of a company who are causing some of their own fake work, but they are probably victims of an outdated practice as well. This large service company hired Carl, a colleague of ours, to help them increase sales. Here's Carl's story:

WRITING PROPOSALS AND SELLING
ARE NOT THE SAME THING

I was hired by a new division of a large Fortune 1000 company. Rewards were generous and were a great recruiting tool for eager young salespeople. The employees were eager and aggressive. But performance was subpar and turnover was remarkably high.

The salespeople responded to over 2,000 RFPs (requests for proposals) each year, which is extraordinary for any business. They won about 5 percent of the bids, or about a hundred. Due to the size of the resulting contracts, the company was surviving, but on very thin margins. Sales managers were in a quandary.

I looked at all the data and talked to every manager and every salesperson. Then I focused on the proposal process—especially the number of proposals the sales team was drafting. I asked some simple questions:

- Why so many?
- Had they analyzed the losses?
- How strategically focused were the RFPs they were responding to?
- How strategic were the ones they were winning?
- What would the financial outcome be if the company submitted only half as many proposals but won 10 percent of the bids because they focused strategically and prioritized opportunities? (They liked that question.)

I suggested they should cut down on the proposals and work to increase the win ratio because they could see extraordinary financial benefits just by reducing workload alone. I also suggested scoring the proposals on a scale to develop a "go or no-go" strategy for responding to the RFPs to ensure they were working on the most valuable opportunities. Sales managers felt that was a big risk and that without 2,000 bids they couldn't maintain their sales goals.

I analyzed the overall burden of the proposal process on the sales team and the management team. The biggest problem was that management focused on the wins, which they celebrated and rewarded generously. They paid little attention to the losses because, well, they didn't have time. Up to 60 percent of the sales team's time was spent on writing proposals—95 percent of which led nowhere.

We learned that they probably had no chance of winning about 30 percent of the bids. Potential clients were using them to justify going with another offer—but in what would appear to be an "open" bid. Another 20 percent of the bids weren't worth winning because they would cause serious delivery problems.

The salespeople were trying to force themselves into sales opportunities. And they weren't facing the fact that proposals don't sell anything. They needed to focus on client relationships. Their writing time was stealing the relationship time.

Ultimately, we agreed that their goal would be to submit about 580 proposals with a goal to win over 40 percent—or about 235. This would allow them to dramatically increase revenue and decrease unproductive work. Also, winning more with less investment means they would have more money to put into salespeople or on the bottom line.

After months of work, they shifted the sales model, changed the focus to relationship-building, started retraining salespeople, created a bid process that analyzed the value of every RFP, and stopped writing proposals to bid on most of them. Salespeople had to win the right to propose and to dedicate resources to the effort.

One last note: When I looked at why the turnover had been so high, the exit interviews showed that sales professionals had thought the proposal process was stupid and overwhelming and that the rewards, regardless of how high, couldn't make up for the pressure and the senselessness of the workload.

Notice how hard people in Carl's story were working and with such good intent. Consider how much time they must have sacrificed to be effective, responsible employees. The company had, somewhere in the process, decided to ignore the aching concern about fake work. The executives had failed to understand the real goals—improving sales by providing the best products that truly served their clients' needs. Instead, they had translated it into the idea that more selling is better selling (more work equals productive work). Of course, this is wrong, but not always easy to see.

Fake Work Negatively Influences Employees and Companies

In the previous example, fake work had serious consequences for both the salespeople and the business as a whole. They were leaving not because of lack of rewards, but because of faulty practices. Our research indicates that 87 percent of workers are not satisfied with the results of their work at the end of most weeks. The gap between real work and fake work is tangible and measurable—and it is the difference between success and failure. Many companies that were once flexible, interesting, and exciting places to work have become disenfranchised, meaningless, bureaucratic morasses that hinder innovation, suck the life force out of people, and produce lots of unprofitable fake work. They've become places where nothing of value seems to get done, and everyone seems to sense it.

Our research shows that no one wants to be doing fake work. (Okay, there may be a few exceptions, but not as many as some cartoons would suggest.) What most of us want is to feel that we're making positive contributions to actual company accomplishments. But not many of us feel we're there. We have found that:

- 87 percent of workers are not satisfied with the results of their work.
- 81 percent of workers do not feel strongly committed to their company's top priorities.

- 68 percent of workers do not feel that their work group goals are translated into real-work tasks.
- Only 52 percent of workers feel they are held accountable for fulfilling their commitments on time.
- 54 percent of all workers feel they have more creativity, resourcefulness, talent, and intelligence than their job requires or allows.
- 53 percent of workers think that the work they do doesn't count for anything.

Statistics like these paint a dispiriting portrait of the individual workers responsible for driving the global economy we're all a part of. And if you look at the company cultures these workers are a part of, the view isn't much better. We have found that:

- 56 percent of workers don't clearly understand their company's most important goals.
- 73 percent of workers don't think their company's goals are translated into specific work they can execute.
- 70 percent of workers don't routinely plan how to support agreed upon goals and tasks in their work groups.

These statistics tell you how and why fake work is infiltrating every work environment—even the best of them. Whether you look at work from the individual's or the company's perspective, what you see is not a pretty—or productive—picture. It isn't that people don't work hard enough; they just don't feel their hard work makes much of a difference to their company. Often they tell us their work is not focused on company strategies. They say they don't know what those strategies are. Our research suggests they're right on all counts.

When we ask about the strategic relevance of their work, individuals typically respond, "What company strategy?" Or they answer, "The strategic work happens in someone else's department, not in mine."

The simple truth is that if people don't know how and why what they do supports their company's strategies, it doesn't matter how hard they work, because their work doesn't connect them to the results that really count.

Fake work erodes one's quality of life and, therefore, a person's devotion and loyalty to any company. When people are assigned a project, wrapped up in a new initiative, or tasked with designing a new marketing campaign only to find out—months later—that all the work they've done has been ignored or, worse, thrown away, it's disheartening and debilitating.

Avoiding the Road to Nowhere: The Pathways Out

In the next chapter, "Exploring the Causes of Fake Work," we will delve more deeply into the environment of fake work. Though it might seem a simple concept, fake work actual exists in a complex world of issues and is eradicated only by awareness, clarity, and sound processes for attacking it.

After we expose the causes, we will examine each of them and provide pathways out—the pathways to real work.

CHAPTER 2
Exploring the Causes of Fake Work

Being busy does not always mean real work. The
object of all work is production or accomplishment
and to either of these ends there must be forethought,
system, planning, intelligence, and honest purpose, as
well as perspiration. Seeming to do is not doing.

— *Thomas Alva Edison*

WHEN YOU BEGIN to understand the concept and accept the existence of fake work, it can feel a little like walking through a minefield—you know it's hidden in places where you least expect it, and knowing that feels a little dangerous. We laugh at the fake work being joked about in *Dilbert* because we all know fakers doing fake work (of course, it's *never* us!). But it's also important to realize how serious the effects of fake work can be. And you have to open your eyes to the causes of fake work before you're able to expel it from your life once and for all.

But before we begin to tiptoe out of the fake-work minefield, let's begin our exploration of the causes of fake work with some basic facts:

- Many, many people, and their actions, cause fake work.
- Many forces have the potential to shift real work to fake work.
- Some people are doing fake work and just don't care.
- Many people don't know they are doing fake work or know that they are causing it.
- Real work is demanding enough. Fake work is eating away at the margins of our sanity.

The following story by Isaac, a manager of a large corporation, covers the gamut of experiences sometimes required in the process of exposing fake work, and it also opens up a barrage of questions about its origins, its nature, and its insidiousness: Specifically, it shows how a planning process affects the streams that join the rivers that cascade down the mountain into a torrent of fake work.

STRATEGY, STRATEGY—WHERE IS THE STRATEGY?

I went with our company leaders on a retreat to the Big Island of Hawaii. The itinerary included a week of golf, strategic thinking, beaches, strategic planning, Hawaiian dancers, and the development of a strategic plan for the company. It was a great week. We bonded. We played some bad golf on a great course. We pounded out big ideas. We filled walls with huge sheets of paper that reflected our best thinking. We agreed on big changes—important changes that would enable us to be competitive and to thrive.

After our week in paradise, we returned home. We immediately got our best writers, our best graphic artists, our best thinkers together to create a prizewinning strategic document, although we immediately wished we had not left all our wallpaper in Hawaii, since we had to re-create our big ideas from random notes from a variety of people. Good stuff got lost forever. That was tough. But we forged ahead and finished our document. It took several weeks of combined effort, but we did it!

Then we reviewed it once, twice. We re-reviewed it a third and fourth time. We circulated it to all the executives who had been there in Hawaii, but deadlines and expectations slipped and slipped—all understandable given the important, busy people who were reviewing it. The process stretched out. We hadn't really expected to complete it quickly—we knew the process would be iterative and introspective over time—but the momentum was starting to fade like the sunsets we had enjoyed from our veranda on the Big Island.

Nine months later, we still didn't have anything to hand out to the employees. People throughout the company were asking about (or having side conversations about) the work done at the executive retreat and the strategic document that had been widely announced as forthcoming and promoted as the game plan for anticipated changes and refocusing of priorities within the company. The delays caused a lot of consternation at lower levels because managers all over the country were waiting for the new plan and wanted to know how it would affect their teams. And their team members felt they were in the dark about what they would be doing when the "new day" dawned.

Feeling the pressure from our peers and our employees and their expectations for the strategic plan, we took another retreat to a nearby resort. We worked—hard. We plowed through the strategic problems and the growth opportunities, and we agreed on most of the lingering issues. We had a lot of catch-up to do, as circumstances had changed since our last strategy session. We wrapped it up.

This time I took ownership myself and saw to it that we published our "prizewinning" strategic plan. Our group then sent it to the leadership team with the expectation that they would present it to their people in the various divisions and teams over the next couple of weeks. We were pleased—finally a plan was in place. Or was it?

Seven months later, I attended a meeting in Atlanta. Someone in the group stood up and asked, "Whatever happened to the plan developed in Hawaii? We heard big things were coming, but we haven't seen or heard anything since." Everyone must have seen me shudder. I gave a one-minute overview of the work and tried to bridge the obvious gulf between our work and the employees' expectations. Several people noted that there had been little communication and that nobody had made it clear what was going on.

I couldn't turn to Harold, my colleague who was supposed to have distributed the plans, because he was no longer at this division. I did check with Annette, the new director who had taken over for him, and I found out that Harold had never sent out the strategic plan to anyone. He hadn't communicated anything. He hadn't brought Annette into the loop. Later, we found a large stack of plans—our grand plans—on a shelf gathering dust.

I checked around—a lot—after that to see if anyone had received the document in other parts of the company. Perhaps 15 percent of our workforce had seen or heard of the plan. We found a few small pockets of people where a senior sponsor had taken the plan to the managers. Even in those cases, the handoff was poor and the dissemination was worse. Many leaders had just stacked the documents on a shelf somewhere, just like Harold. Nothing had changed. We weren't falling into a hole or anything; business was moving along. But all the strategies, all the directional changes that our employees were *expecting*, were either ignored or unheard of.

The above story oozes with fake work. Fake work seems to be built into the culture of the company, beginning with a retreat where the work was fake and the play was real. More problematic is the behavior of senior leadership, which seems to promote a fake-work standard of long hours, big commitments, lots of talk, little execution, even less follow-through, no alignment, and minimal communication. However, by diagnosing the causes and then addressing solutions, we may find the pathways to real work, real value, and real contributions that make sense to us and to those we work with.

A Diagnostic Process:
Finding the Causes of Fake Work

The examination of productivity will likely always be a corporate practice. Quality Control, TQM (Total Quality Management), Zero Defects, Six Sigma, and other process improvement methods focus on work and productivity and the efficiencies of every single work process. But, as a Six Sigma expert told us, "the problem is that we haven't always asked all the right questions up front, such as: Is this the work we should be doing?" The key is to be aware of and ask the right questions from the start. And bear in mind that fake work creeps even into companies with remarkable focus. How worrisome must that be for the rest?

As we try to identify the common causes of fake work, we must remember that they have common roots that can be found in three simple yet significant questions:

- Am I sure I am doing real work?
- Do I know and understand the importance of my work to the mission, vision, goals, and strategies of my company?
- Is my work critical? How critical? Why?

All of the causes we will explore are byproducts of not knowing the answers to these questions at four basic levels: individual, team, management and leadership, and the company or organization. Here's how things can break down at each level:

1. *Yes, causes can begin with you.* You may be on the wrong track, not paying attention, or clueless about whether your work connects to company goals. Perhaps you are unwilling to take new directions. Maybe you are stuck and "just want to do your job," and maybe you are reaping the rewards of fake work.

2. *The causes have a team aspect.* When you fail to work with your team members, you duplicate tasks, fail to communicate, and work on the wrong things. Teams often fail to align with strategies and fail to execute tasks crucial to company goals because the members are unknowingly working against each other or against other teams in the company.

3. *Managers and leaders can set fake work in motion.* You can steer people clearly and set up the opportunities for alignment and execution, but too often you set up or allow for the conditions of fake work.

4. *Companies can establish environments where fake work creeps into the systems, structures, and processes that affect work throughout the enterprise.* When companies fail to clarify their goals, they set up a beehive of activity that is really just fake work.

If you are asking the right questions about fake work and are aware of how people in every level of the company contribute to fake work, you should have a different perspective about the workplace. Here are ten of the leading causes why companies are plagued with fake work.

Cause 1. Failing to Understand Your Job—Your Real Job

Simply put, do you know what you should be doing—*really doing*—at work because your company *really* needs you to do it? This may seem like a simple question, but it is frightening how many people don't actually understand the difference between what we think we should be doing and what our companies need us to be doing.

If, as our research indicates, 81 percent of workers feel no strong commitment to their company's top priorities, then employees either don't care about company priorities or they don't know what they are—or a combination of the two. We have a basic belief that most people want to do work of value that brings value to their company. So, many problems arise because they aren't paying attention to their company's goals and strategies, don't know what the goals and strategies are, or don't know the right questions to ask from the get-go, since they don't actually understand what their job is.

A good deal of fake work is caused by out-of-date job descriptions for a job that has changed dramatically. Another cause is that people don't ask and therefore aren't told that their job is now bigger or more complex or requires different skills. We have heard a hundred stories about people in jobs that were very different from what they thought they got hired to do. Terry Ann told us:

SAFETY IS JOB 1

I was hired to monitor the flow of bottles to trucks in a warehouse. I was kind of a combination of traffic cop and guard dog. I was told, many times, that things worked better if I stayed out of the way. Then one day, a pallet dropped off a forklift and pinned Morris, an employee, to the ground. It was a miracle that he wasn't killed. I had no authority, no duty, to solve safety problems, but I was blamed for Morris's injury anyway. That was the first time I realized that, to save my job, I really needed to manage conflicts, troubleshoot processes, and oversee safety. When I told my boss that I needed to change my focus, he said, "Well, yeah!" Clearly that was his way of saying, "It's about time," even though everything I had been told up to that point was the opposite of his expectations.

Very often, the underlying cause of people's failure to understand their jobs is how many assumptions they make. For example, you might have been hired for a job with the title of manager's assistant so you think you are supposed to be assisting. But your boss thinks you ought to be solving contracting issues. That is a big difference. Another person told us that he was hired right out of college to do a marketing job, but it turned out to be a sales position. Although he liked the challenge and he needed the job, he did fake work for months because he didn't understand sales at all—and no one bothered to explain to him what was expected of him. The cost of not understanding what your job is can be high—in Terry Ann's case, it almost cost someone his life.

Cause 2. Failing to Recognize the Finish Line

In many ways, work is a lot like running the 26.2 miles of a marathon. That's a daunting task even for a well-trained runner, but imagine the challenge if as the starting gun goes off, you're not quite sure where the finish line is! In the same manner, a common cause of fake work is that many employees don't understand the results that they should be shooting for and when they are expected to achieve them.

If you know what your job is, then you should know its purpose. And the purpose always focuses on a result. So, if you understand the results you're after, you should have the finish line firmly in mind. There's an optimistic side of us that asks: *Doesn't everyone undertake or assign work with the finish line in mind?* The truth is: Not necessarily! Given that potential for breakdown, when you are first assigned a task, you should ask your supervisor these questions:

1. What is the result you are seeking?
2. Why is my assignment important?
3. When do you want it completed?

Too many of us either forget to ask or totally ignore these critical questions, so we guess wrong or we don't even guess at all. Which is obviously detrimental to the result and the company. Josie, a young college-age woman, shared this story:

FINDING THE OUTCOMES INHERENT IN THE WORK

I was working in a really nice restaurant that was losing its spark—and its reputation. All the employees seemed apathetic about their work. The head chef would tell me, again and again, that he was just working to work. He had other plans, which involved quitting and opening his own restaurant someday. And all the cooks seemed to follow his lead with poor attitudes. Complaints were multiplying about the food, regular customers weren't returning, and the restaurant was losing money.

Dylan, the owner, assembled the staff one evening for a talk. Fighting off tears, he told us: "I am going to lose this place and my house along with it. I think you are all working just so you can get paid, but you have totally forgotten why you are here. You have lost your passion and don't seem to understand our one clear goal: thrilled customers! Without them, we are out of business. We can't keep them without greeting them enthusiastically and joyfully, seating them promptly, and making them feel welcome by attending to them immediately, helping them enjoy the experience, serving them constantly and joyously, and providing them with food that is unforgettable. So, if you can't help us get those results, please leave before you kill me and lose your soul in the process."

Everyone was stunned—mostly because we had never seen Dylan's passion, but also because we had lost sight of the reasons for coming to work. In about one minute, Dylan had helped everyone see both of the intended outcomes of our work: profit and passion. That night, the restaurant began to change, and it was the start of a real turnaround.

Josie's story is an excellent example of the importance of understanding the reasons for the work we do. However, the finish line is often more elusive than the one in the above story. Most of us are working in roles that require a lot of change and adaptation. And in the midst of all that, tasks change, priorities change, and the finish line gets blurred. So remember the three questions, and if you're still unsure where the finish line lies, keep asking.

Cause 3. Failing to Focus and Prioritize

To avoid falling into a deep, dark fake-work hole, you need to ask this question often—and repeatedly: Out of the many, many things that you *can* be doing, what are the few critical things that you *must* be doing? This question will help you maintain your foothold in the world of real work, and ensure that you are adding real value to your company. The following story illustrates how a careless manager can trap an employee in a mass of tasks while something critical falls through the cracks. This story, shared by Justine, tells how Mike got trapped.

AIRPLANES SLIPPING THROUGH THE CRACKS

I was the administrative assistant for a service products group in a company that sold jet engines. Mike was the best worker in the group—he was smart and dedicated. The company was in a big push to shift its focus from products to services—meaning that the company made more profit on service items, like repair kits, than on the engines. Mike had one big problem—he was such a hard worker that more and more work just kept coming his way.

Nearly crazy, Mike met with his boss, Stewart, to review his work plans and discuss priorities. He was feeling overwhelmed with so many key things to pay attention to because of this service initiative. Stewart said that he didn't know what was most important, but that Mike should know. Stewart just told him dismissively, "Figure it out, but don't drop anything. Right now, everything is important."

So Mike worked on service packages for all the group's customers. He wrote e-mails to all the customers to track their service plans. He revised pricing models and updated pricing sheets. He did forecasting. He worked with a team on a communication plan to stay connected to their customers. Mike worked on new processes for shipping and new procedures for handling customer calls. He set up training on the shift. He was mowing down tasks, hoping that things would get caught up soon.

One Friday at 5 p.m., just as Mike was getting ready to walk out for a much-needed weekend, Stewart walked in, glared at Mike and yelled, "You idiot, you stupid idiot! We just learned that maintenance kits didn't get out of the warehouse and twenty-one airplanes were grounded for the day. Legal tells us that our company is responsible for millions of dollars of lost revenue, and they're drowning in customer complaints and threats. So pack up your things—you're fired."

I learned about it the following Monday. It was hard because I knew the truth. Stewart hadn't told Mike that the kits were the number one priority—it was just one of the many items on his list. Also, Mike thought Laurie's team was sending out the maintenance kits on a routine basis, while Laurie thought the work had been shifted to Mike. In all of this work to drive the new initiative, the heart of the business got left off everyone's critical job list. Stewart knew the kits were top priority, and he just assumed that everyone knew. Mike lost his job and Stewart had someone to blame for it.

Mike's nightmare illustrates just one of many problems that surface when priorities aren't sorted out, when people aren't talking, when *busyness overwhelms emphasis.* Too often, people like Stewart assume that everyone understands what is going on and has the same information. But Mike and Laurie weren't innocent, either. Everyone was careless and working hard on many things from the B and C lists. Furthermore, when all work is treated as equal, fake work is an inevitable outcome. Watch out when you are facing one or more of these key problems:

1. You don't know the difference between nonessential tasks and critical tasks.
2. You haven't prioritized or asked your supervisor about the priority of your tasks.
3. You, along with your team, aren't negotiating the number of tasks each person is doing or discussing the priority items, and which ones need to rise to the top and which ones need to drop from the list.
4. When you do ask about priorities, your supervisor gives you the wrong answers because he doesn't actually know which tasks are priorities.
5. When you ask supervisors to help prioritize, they just add tasks to your lists, and you agree to them.

Fake work prospers in any environment where employees at any level are uncertain about the priorities associated with expectations, products, outcomes, and deadlines. Failing to prioritize is a major cause of fake work because we find ourselves spreading our effort over from high-level to low-level tasks and because we lose passion for work that gets mediocre results and lackluster feedback.

Cause 4. Failing to Understand the People Around You

People, whether they have good intentions or bad, cause fake work, and in any situation, the interactions between people add challenges and complexity to the workplace. As one saleswoman told us, "I like sales, and if I didn't have to deal with people it would be great." That is a problem that most of us can relate to. People have different ways of thinking and acting, different ways of defining their personal values and goals, and different ways of rationalizing and justifying their personal choices. Those differences affect us and the work we do, and add a layer of complexity to our battle with fake work.

Before we embark on our battle, however, we must begin to understand how the people we work with contribute to the fake work we're a part of. Consider a few examples.

- "Henry hasn't completed a project in the two years I have been here. He has a knack for handing off projects and moving to something new just when the work gets hard and accountability is on the line."
- "I worked for Reggie, a very smart manager who gets caught up in lots of new ideas, but gets us in trouble every year because he totally forgets the bottom-line business issues."
- "When Jonah gets angry, he pulls the energy of the whole team. Our group spends hours coping with his lack of control. Our loss of focus gets us further off track and will lead, inevitably, to another blowup."
- "Janice invents new projects to prop up her reputation, but they distract us from our work. I guess it helps her, but it's killing us."
- "I am great at getting exactly what I want. I can convince

my boss every time that I have a breakthrough idea, and I get to run my own little fiefdom for months."

These quotes are about or from people who can and will—with or without negative intentions—contribute to the fake work you're caught up in. We live in a multicultural, diverse world filled with people with differing attitudes, differing needs, and a multitude of personality traits that can prevent us from doing our best work. People who are not results-oriented, who are isolationists, egocentrics, and obsessive organizers, also affect you and can create fake work. One manager may think that his anger is motivating workers; another may think her incessant and iterative process is adding value. The key is to be able to recognize how other people's behavior can cause you fake work, and to figure out how to work with them without falling into the fake-work traps they're setting. Equally important, and possibly more difficult, is assessing whether *you* are the one who is causing your coworkers fake work.

First, you must confront yourself—identify your attitudes, needs, and personality traits so you better understand your impact on others. Then you can try to understand others and your relationships with them. People bring their different personalities, skills, knowledge, and attributes to a team. That diversity can increase the value of the team, but it can also threaten its harmony and effectiveness.

Cause 5. Failing to Communicate About the Right Things

Any time the wrong work is being done—people are following the wrong schedule, focusing on the wrong project, or giving a task the wrong amount of effort—a lack of communication is one of the causes. Bad communication will always be one of the biggest causes of fake work.

There are many elements of miscommunication and the examples are endless, but a communication breakdown has likely caused fake work in your workplace if you hear comments like these:

- "I didn't know that we had changed our service model. I hadn't heard anything about it. And I never saw the e-mail my boss was talking about."
- "I don't know anything about any pricing change."
- "We are struggling with our coordination of resources, and we never talk about it."
- "Our manager gets involved in project reviews, budget analysis, sales, and program management. But what we need her to do is communicate about expectations and facilitate overall discussion from team to team."
- "He didn't tell us anything about the goals our home office had in place until we failed to meet them."

Company leaders often tell us they have worked hard to communicate strategy and get people connected, yet we often find that they have almost totally failed. People didn't see it, didn't read it, didn't hear it, didn't understand it, or just ignored it.

But everyone plays a part in that ineffective equation. Communication is a communal task. It requires more than one party. You can't just send communication out; you must know if it was heard and understood. And even with all our modern technology, the communication loop can be harder to close than we think. In fact, many conveniences like cell phones, BlackBerrys, and access to e-mail at all hours create a glut of information that overwhelms communication rather than facilitating it. Along with the technology, many other patterns of the modern work environment—working with headphones, working at home, working on weekends—creates isolation and weakens communication channels.

Cause 6. Failing to Understand the Importance of Your Team

Teams are the vital organs of most work environments. While you are responsible for many individual tasks, they are performed through the lens of a team. And one of the biggest causes of fake work is that teams do not work cohesively. Sports metaphors are easy to call on because often sports teams illustrate the purity of teams: Members have very specific *and* common purposes, pull together to support each other, work toward common goals, and ultimately serve the needs of their sponsoring organization— school, community, or owner—and fulfill the needs of the fans (or end users). Given the importance of teams in the workplace, we are surprised how often we hear comments like these from individuals within the same team:

1. "I didn't know you did that."
2. "I've never known what you did all day."
3. "I thought I was supposed to be doing that."
4. "I haven't talked to her in months."
5. "We have team meetings, but we never talk about strategies."
6. "We don't have team meetings; our manager meets with each of us and tells each of us slightly different things about what is most important."

The fact is, a lot of team members and supervisors don't have a clue about the real value and intent of their teams. And they don't know how or even why they need to get their teams working together.

When companies tell us that they are providing team-building exercises, too often they tell us about the ropes course or the horseback riding excursions that are designed to pull teams together. We see nothing wrong with helping people get to know each other and do something together outside of work—but in the end, they have to go back to work and (supposedly) work together. And often, back at work, nobody is doing any team-building at all. Teams will work much better together when they talk about and solve the problems of their work together—as a team.

It's easy to see the problem when companies create silos that separate teams and hurt integration and sharing. But even within teams, individuals can also work in silos—or offices and cubicles— without understanding or considering the importance of teamwork. The following story illustrates what happens when members of a team work in individual silos. The story comes from Jonah, who works in a refinery.

SECRETS REVEALED

I was assigned to work on documentation about managing hazardous chemicals as required by law. I collected every detail that I could. I met with many key people. I spent months writing. It was one of the hardest projects I had ever taken on. At first I thought it was assigned to me as some kind of punishment, but my boss told me that she really needed me to do this work, and I felt good about the confidence she had in me.

Just as I was coming down the homestretch, I was in a team meeting. Carla, one of my coworkers, asked about the project that had buried me for so long. After I told her what I'd been working on, she said, "I may have something that will help." After lunch, she brought me a box of materials—including a manual that had about two-thirds of the content that I had spent weeks creating. Some of it filled in gaps, some of it validated my work, and some of it showed me where I was off track. Regardless, I felt sick. I had dedicated months to redundant, useless work. If I had only asked my team members a few questions, I could have completed my task in a couple of weeks rather than several months.

You should appreciate the fact that you are usually surrounded by smart, helpful people who can assist you in solving and working through problems. When you learn to take advantage of their knowledge and abilities, you will distance yourself from fake work. But more important, when you and your team have learned to work together to clarify jobs and critical tasks, to prioritize and negotiate those tasks, to define the results and the deadlines, and to communicate regularly and diligently, you will make huge steps forward as a team and in your own professional life.

Cause 7. Failing to Clarify and Drive Strategy from Top to Bottom

When you don't know or understand strategies and the processes required to implement them, you're likely to end up with fake work. A huge cause of fake work is that companies create and develop strategies that workers never learn about. As noted previously, our research shows that *73 percent of workers don't think their company's goals are translated into specific work they can execute.*

That statistic tells us a couple of things. First, it tells us that the work involved in creating strategy is often fake work because this often costly, arduous, complex work is not getting into the hands and minds of employees.

Second, if many—perhaps most—employees are not shifting their work and their focus toward critical, strategic changes, fake work is emanating from every pore of the company.

Smart companies don't let that happen. Smart managers drive key strategies forward, and smart teams and individuals make sure they understand and translate strategies into their work. But unfortunately, strategy implementation can still break down, even if you have only one weak link in the corporate chain. Fake work starts with:

- Poorly articulated and poorly focused strategies.
- Plans that are poorly written, too long, and hard to read and understand.
- Plans that are shared with managers without assurance that they understand the reasoning and the expectations.
- Plans that are not shared with teams and individuals across the company.
- Plans that are ignored because of apathy, mistrust, doubt, or lack of guidance.

Strategies require focus and attention. When companies don't focus on their strategies effectively, don't communicate them effectively, and don't align their employees with them effectively, they are putting the entire enterprise at risk.

Cause 8. Failing to See the Execution Gap—Alignment, Then Execution

You can have an excellent strategy, but if not everyone within the company is aligned to that strategy, then fake work ensues. Our research shows that *80 percent of all change processes fail because they are not implemented properly.* Strategic planning is not a thing; it is a process—a change process. Implementation is the process of rolling out strategy from the top of the company to the bottom, where it is executed effectively, but alignment is all about individuals linking their work tasks to strategy and taking responsibility for them.

The implementation process can break down at many points, but a common point is at the team level because of a lack of alignment. We call this the execution gap. The execution gap is the quicksand in the gulf between the strategies a company seeks to implement and what people actually do. And that gulf is closed by alignment, which is the matching of people with the tasks that need to be done.

We have discussed many of the failings of executives and managers to get strategy in place and to start rolling it out, but alignment is not a leadership issue—it is a team and a personal issue. In fact, a fatal flaw of leaders is that they think they can align people. People aren't machines that can be adjusted like the alignment of your car tires. People have to align themselves. You cannot rid your world of fake work without understanding this critical concept: *Fake work is work that is not strategically aligned.* Sylvia, a marketing manager, put it this way:

GETTING ON THE SAME PAGE

When our team got together to discuss how we would help drive the new strategy, no two people were on the same page.

Some didn't understand the plan to present our new service package to our customers, some didn't even know there was a new package, some were unsure of their roles. I thought I had gotten everyone focused on their tasks, but clearly they didn't see the tasks in the context of strategic focus for the company. Hours later, everyone adjusted their focus, rethought their work, formed new teams, and determined how the team would drive the strategy forward.

Once people align themselves with strategy, the other aspects of work come together much more readily. All value comes at the point of work—executing work in alignment with the most important goals of the company. Without alignment you have no point to work and a pool of fake workers.

Alignment is a team process. It requires that people work together with their coworkers, managers, and leaders to adjust, adapt, negotiate, and focus the work of each person with every other person. The main element crucial to successful alignment is communication. It requires careful listening, translating strategy to tasks, understanding business needs, and adapting to new circumstances.

In the end, execution is the culmination of precise actions focused on getting the results the company seeks. We are each critical to the ultimate success of our companies, regardless of our roles. If we are aligned and executing effectively, we have a chance to make a difference in our own lives and in our companies.

Cause 9. Failing to Manage—No Matter Our Level

Managers are a primary cause of fake work because their role is, by design, to serve as a conduit for meaning. Strategies and results flow through that conduit, and fake work comes out the other end when information is translated incorrectly, ignored, or not passed on at all.

But before you slip into the temptation to pass all blame for fake work to your manager, remember that every employee, whether at the top of the corporate ladder or the bottom—plays some role in oversight, decision making, communication, and the effectiveness or failure of management. It is easy to blame managers for clogging up the conduit, but we each must help improve our work environment if our companies are to be successful.

Whatever your role in management, you are causing fake work if you are *not*:

- Keenly aware of the company's most important strategies and the results you need to target.
- Doing your part to facilitate communication about those strategies, either as the one sharing information or the one receiving it.
- Clarifying the most critical work, either for yourself as you interact with your manager or for those you manage.
- Helping prioritize and focus work.
- Checking, again and again, to see how you can remove obstacles to success.

Whether they involve managing a project or a team or a task, these key elements remain the same. Management is about facilitation, translation, mentoring, coaching, and aiding the ability of others to succeed. And whether managing or being managed, we each play a part in the process.

Cause 10. Failing to See That Culture Creates an Environment of Fake Work

All the causes mentioned above work interdependently—each contributing its own part to the mix of fake work. Fake work grows out of a thousand places brought about by a thousand stimuli. But fake work prospers in cultures that are not self-aware. Many companies have had to make themselves over. Great companies continue to hone the best of their cultures and build an environment of success.

Building a corporate culture is an organic process. It may have started somewhere with a single leader or a small group and grown over time, but it can, and often needs to, change. That means that everyone can begin to affect cultures in an exciting way.

A company's culture comprises its people, systems, structures, and processes; its mission, vision, and objectives; and its standards, policies, and procedures. But mostly, a company's culture is built from the values and behaviors of the individuals within the company—the informal attitudes and ethics and ideas that each person brings and expects of one another. A culture can frame an environment of focus, passion, clarity, and vitality. But it can also fuel doubt, suspicion, confusion—and immense amounts of fake work. Of course, most companies fall somewhere in between.

Shifts in company cultures happen all the time. Stodgy old-world companies have adjusted to be more agile to attract young people and to focus new attention on new ideas. And hotshot, laid-back companies have learned that they need some controls in place to manage all that youthful exuberance.

The flaws—sometimes fatal flaws—occur when companies don't pay enough attention to who they are and how they behave. Sometimes something in the culture is controlling, ruling the environment, that a company may not even recognize: tradition, the strong personality of a CEO, the overpowering essence of a looming competitor who dominates the market, stockholders, and employees. This can be extremely detrimental to a company if it's not brought to light and addressed. Surely, many businesses survive on the strength of their products, but if something is poisoning the culture, it's still just a house of cards. Consider a company in California that had 85 percent of the market with its very targeted technical instrumentation. One senior leader told us:

MONEY BLOWING INTO THE STREETS

We are doing so much business right now that if you open any door, money will blow into the streets. But we don't do many things very well. We are struggling with all the details—

systems, structures, and processes—and will get worse as we grow. I am not sure what we are doing with all the money we're making. I don't know if we are, in the long run, going to have any money left over. I am afraid that a competitor that gets the work done right and has a strong infrastructure will put us out of business overnight.

This story illustrates a business that is surviving on a market need, but may be dying because fake work is bleeding the company to death. Businesses like these excel with a product that hits a market niche, and they usually have smart people who help them take off, but they cannot sustain their growth without the systems, structures, and processes that build a stable company. They must create those so they support the growth and their customers, or they will end up with pockets of excellence throughout the company that barely survive within an institution of fake work.

People do not like fake work. People will change to help build and improve a culture that is besieged by problems that don't seem likely to go away. Jim Collins's book *Good to Great* profiles companies that have remade themselves and found new vigor and different standards for approaching their problems. These are companies paying attention to their culture.

Ultimately, knowing and understanding the causes of fake work gives you options for knowing how to respond to them. As we explore the Pathways to Real Work, we hope you will find valuable solutions to attack the fake work that may be stealing your sense of value. These pathways provide a platform for making courageous and valuable choices: pursuing the truth about your work, solving a team problem, challenging your supervisor, prodding your company, and changing roles or jobs.

PART 2

The Pathways out of Fake Work

PATH 1

Discovering Your World of Fake Work

We are either doing something or we are not.
"Talking about" is a subset of "not."

—*from* The Office *website*

MANY PEOPLE HAVE no idea how much of their time is spent doing fake work. Path 1: Discovering Your World of Fake Work stresses the importance of self-discovery. To discover your personal fake-work profile, take the test on Page 48. It will help you to start thinking about your participation in fake work.

Further, on this path you'll learn four steps that will help avoid and prevent fake work:

Step 1: Be vigilant in looking for signs of fake work.
Step 2: Weigh your work against your company's strategic goals.
Step 3: Do it now to avoid fake work.
Step 4: Realize that grasping reality drives real work.

Path 1 is important because, as with a hidden disease, the symptoms of fake work might not be manifesting themselves. You can be feeling great and enjoying life. Then, you go to the doctor and discover that you have a serious health problem that has sneaked up on you without obvious symptoms or warnings. You might protest to the doctor: "But I haven't had any problems with my body. I don't have any symptoms."

A fake-work diagnosis can be similar. You can be working hard, and you know you are being a good employee. But then an adviser or specialist helps you discover that you are doing mostly fake work. This discovery is the first step in dealing with your fake-work affliction. And, like an illness, when you know what the problem is, you have a chance to overcome it. We hope to help you diagnose your fake-work problems and treat them as quickly as possible.

Here's an example of why it is so important to discover and deal with your fake work early on in your job.

HARD WORK CAN BE FAKE WORK

Deb was hired to be a senior training director at a large company. When she was hired she was encouraged to make certain she focused on training "that would make a difference." Having recently completed her master's in instructional design, Deb knew how to develop training exercises that got participants involved, and her early efforts got great evaluations from the participants.

During her first year Deb and her team developed four state-of-the-art courses in sales, management, leadership, and communication. Deb's group taught each course ten times during her first year with the company, earning ratings of 4.9 out of 5 for both the courses and the teaching. Deb was working hard and her team members were killing themselves, but she was very pleased with their work.

When Deb reported her success to the CEO, he thanked her for all her hard work and congratulated her on such fine ratings from the participants. Then he said to her frankly, "But even after all these courses, our turnover is down, our sales per person haven't improved, our work processes aren't any more effective. Deb, the training you're doing is good only if it is making a difference to our organization and our strategic goals. If it doesn't improve our bottom line, it doesn't matter."

After their talk, Deb hired a measurement firm to evaluate the impact of her work based on the organization's strategic goals. And the CEO's skepticism proved well founded: Despite all the hard work by Deb and her team, turnover had gone up, sales had gone down, and the organization was doing even worse than before the new courses started. The consultants explained to Deb that although she had clearly been working hard, her work didn't matter—because her training program had failed to bring about changes that would improve the bottom line.

Deb and the consultants looked at the courses and identified all the elements that weren't strategically connected— that is, not linked with the most important business issues. She refocused her efforts and retooled every course to drive business goals. She worked with the business leaders in each of the company's divisions to ensure that critical issues were addressed. She rebuilt exercises to make them relevant and applicable. She quickly learned that while it is much harder to create real-work training, it is vastly more rewarding both to the company and to the individual.

Deb's story illustrates the importance of being on the lookout for fake work even when you feel like you're firing on all cylinders.

What to Know About Path 1

To help you begin to evaluate whether you do fake work or real work, take this short test:

THE FAKE WORK SIGNS TEST

Rate the following statements on a scale of 1 to 5, with 5 meaning totally true and 1 totally false.

Statement	Select Only One False True
1. I don't fully understand my position's job description.	1 2 3 4 5 ☐ ☐ ☐ ☐ ☐
2. Much of the work I do each day does not match my job description.	1 2 3 4 5 ☐ ☐ ☐ ☐ ☐
3. I don't know the strategic goals of my company.	1 2 3 4 5 ☐ ☐ ☐ ☐ ☐
4. My job description is not clearly connected to the strategic goals of my company.	1 2 3 4 5 ☐ ☐ ☐ ☐ ☐
5. My hard work does not seem to achieve the results that matter to my company.	1 2 3 4 5 ☐ ☐ ☐ ☐ ☐
6. The meetings I hold or attend do not have clear purposes.	1 2 3 4 5 ☐ ☐ ☐ ☐ ☐
7. I work on assignments that no one seems to care about.	1 2 3 4 5 ☐ ☐ ☐ ☐ ☐
8. I give out assignments that take time but do not appear to influence company results.	1 2 3 4 5 ☐ ☐ ☐ ☐ ☐
9. I attend company training programs that are nice but don't seem to make a difference to the company's success.	1 2 3 4 5 ☐ ☐ ☐ ☐ ☐
10. Much of the work I do is not directly related to the success of my company.	1 2 3 4 5 ☐ ☐ ☐ ☐ ☐

Add up the numbers represented by your responses.

A "perfect" score of 50 indicates that you are doing 100 percent fake work. The lowest possible score, 10, means the work you're doing is 100 percent real. In our work with many companies, we have found that the average score falls between 25 and 35, which suggests that most people spend about half of their time doing fake work. A score above 35 suggests that most of your time is spent doing fake work, and a score of 25 or lower suggests that you work in an environment that does very little fake work.

Awakening to Fake Work

The questions in the quiz may have reminded you of a time when you've been rudely awakened to the fact that you were doing fake work and were suffering from its dehumanizing effects. Have any of the following happened to you?

- Somebody asked you to spend two hours every week compiling status reports that would be shoved into a folder and never looked at again.
- You were put on an action team to drive a customer service initiative only to find out that its authority was superseded by a different team tasked with the same objective.
- You were asked to help out with an HR project designed to boost morale that consisted of taking pictures of people at work and setting up "happy employee" photo montages on every available bulletin board. You later discovered that employees regularly mocked and jeered at the pictures.
- The team you were managing was targeted to be merged into another department, and you realized that many of the people on your team would likely lose their jobs. But no leader in the company was willing to officially say what was happening. So, when you should have been helping these employees transition to a new team or new jobs, you instead gave them tasks that probably amounted to fake work.

These awakenings to fake work can trigger a variety of responses: malaise, fear, ill will about your colleagues, and a sense of dread about the next twenty or thirty years you'll be forced to spend in the workforce. Government work is often singled out for its waste and meaninglessness, and we agree. However, we often fail to recognize the same telltale signs of fake and dehumanizing work in private-sector offices and organizations as well. Bureaucratic work is everywhere, and no one is insulated from the threat of fake work.

The Modern Workplace Is Saturated in Fake Work

Fake work is so common that it's made pop culture hits out of comic strips like "Dilbert," films like *Swimming with Sharks* and *Office Space*, and TV shows like *The Office*. It happens all across the organizational chart, and even though there's always real work to be done, we've witnessed the exponential growth and spread of fake work firsthand in our own careers—through layoffs that targeted the wrong groups of people, trivial projects that cascade down the levels of an organization, or an upper-level management team so caught up in its own pet project that it drives its organization into the ground.

Fake work reaches out to include everyone from the inattentive CEO who changes strategy too frequently, to the social-climbing manager who creates busywork to make herself look important, to the shirking line worker who just doesn't want to do anything today. Fake work is done by diligent, hard-working people and by people who try to avoid real work at all costs and end up passing the fake buck to others. Probably the greatest generator of fake work is employees and their leaders who don't regularly review the work they are doing and its relationship to company strategy. Fake work is continued by workers who get so caught up in their tasks that they forget to question whether the work is really what the company needs.

Fake Work May Be a Fact, But It Doesn't Have to Be Permanent

Fake work is a fundamental aspect of every workplace—often, more than half of the work done qualifies as fake work—and therefore you must learn to deal with it. You should not avoid it by burying your head in the sand or your face in a pint of Ben & Jerry's every night trying to forget how you've spent your day. You must confront it by recognizing it and by avoiding it whenever possible. The good news is that avoiding fake work is simple to achieve: You can do meaningful work if you *choose* to stop doing fake work and if you make sure that the work you do is always based in the real needs of your company's environment.

If you can't completely stop doing fake work, you can try to reduce the amount of fake work that you do by as much as possible. It's unrealistic to think that everyone could be doing real work 100 percent of the time, but most people should be able to increase the amount of real work they're currently doing. People are surprised at how low the percentage of real work being completed is. Increasing the amount of real work done from 20 percent up to 40 percent or 40 percent up to 70 percent would make a massive change in any company.

Reducing and Avoiding Fake Work

Fake work is all around and hidden in practically every task, so you must constantly be looking for and avoiding it. Sometimes *you* cause it when you hold a meeting and a team of people arrives without purpose and leaves without action items. Sometimes your bosses are asking you to work on tasks that have already been done. How rewarding it would be to devote your effort to real work—work that actually accomplishes something. And we have found that doing real work leads you to do more real work, and the more we are all invested in the reality of our work, the more work becomes meaningful for everyone involved with it.

In our consulting practice, one senior manager, Kevin, shared this classic fake-work anecdote:

RUBBER-STAMPING MERIT INCREASES

As a senior-level manager Kevin was responsible for approving merit increases for a group of employees who were three levels below him on the organizational chart. However, he was never given any criteria for turning down a merit increase.

Increasingly tired of rubber-stamping these merit increases, he finally asked his boss if anyone had ever been denied. The answer: no. Furthermore, the boss indicated that certain union contracts prohibited the company from denying a merit increase without involving Legal in the decision. Any merit increases recommended by a direct supervisor had to be accepted by the organization. In other words, the senior manager was basically making a non-decision to approve a lower-level person's decision. Once he realized the fakeness of the entire situation, he worked to eliminate the extra review cycle and spare himself more fake work.

Of course, not everyone is high enough up the organizational chart to effect the kind of change that this manager did. It's even harder to bring about organization-wide change, and sometimes it's impossible to get out of doing the fake work that higher-level people assign you. But as you discover fake work, you can always choose, on a personal level, to make sure that the tasks you *can* control are aligned to what's real and right.

Though you may not be able to control the flow of fake work above you, you can at least make sure that you send only real work to the people who work for you. If you are told that a project is critical to the organization, you should always ask how and why, though beyond that, the problem of discovering fake work may be hovering far above your level of influence. If you're at the bottom of the organizational chart, we understand that you may not be able to stop fake work from occurring. But anytime you find you are or may be doing fake work, try to stop it. Bring it to your manager's attention. Work it through with your team. We will give you many different ways to address this situation, but you also must find your own ways to fight and eliminate fake work because it hurts you, your manager, and your company in the long run.

How can you move down the path of self-discovery and reduce, eliminate, and avoid as much fake work as possible?

Steps to Move Down Path 1

Step 1. Be Vigilant for Signs of Fake Work

Being vigilant for signs of fake work means, plain and simple, to ask yourself and others constantly whether you are doing fake work. *If I complete my current work assignment, will it lead to real work that moves the company forward? If I do this work, will it support company goals? Do I keep people focused on real work and avoid unproductive fake work?* You must be constantly vigilant about how you spend your time at work.

Being vigilant for signs of fake work means . . .

- Understanding your job. Why does it exist and how does it fit within and serve the organization?
- Keeping your mind focused on what really needs to be done—focus on whether your work is tied to the company's strategic goals.
- Constantly inquiring about the reasons for and value of assignments and projects.
- Assessing the depth and breadth of your work to see if it all matters and if it matters equally.
- Negotiating for real work and making your case against fake work.
- Trying to help every meeting focus on real work.
- Scheduling only purposeful, real-work-oriented meetings and conference calls.
- Choosing to be focused and prioritized rather than passive and lazy.
- Being confident enough to believe in your interpretation of work situations, even when your interpretation differs from other people's, but also understanding and accepting that your perception of a situation is almost always limited or partial.

Being vigilant for signs of fake work is affected by your ability to focus on what you really need to be doing in your work environment. Also, it means understanding that your perception of the situation will always be inherently limited, and that you need to strive to articulate the larger truth of the situation and do what's best for everyone—not just your own personal agenda. Be able to see the larger situation for what it really is, and act accordingly to reduce fake work in your life and in your company.

A word of caution: Be careful not to get overly invested in seeing things through your own particular focal lens, which can be clouded by your pet projects, your paycheck, your political supporters and antagonists. You inevitably end up filtering your perception of a situation to suit your particular needs, instead of assessing honestly whether it involves real work or fake work.

Step 2. Weigh Your Work Against Your Company's Strategic Goals

Remember that real work is productive activity applied to the achievement of organizational goals—the stuff that keeps your organization in business. Work doesn't always need to be DEFCON-1 important, but it does need to be real enough to justify spending your, or someone's, effort in doing it.

We've all been the victims of recycled work, a project that keeps getting bounced around like a hot potato until it lands on someone who can't say no or is given to someone who doesn't realize that it's insignificant work that's been repackaged as "critical." It's the kind of project that takes just as much time—if not more—to explain how to do it than just doing it. By the time it's even two people away from the original source of the request, the project gets bungled because it's usually boring, detail-oriented work that loses touch with the original owner, who knows exactly what he or she wants.

So keep your work real by focusing on activities that lead to organizational productivity. Also, recognize your ability to determine if a certain piece of work leads to productivity, and think before passing along a project that's trivial, or so specific that you'll just end up redoing it after the person you assign it to turns it in.

Step 3. Do It Now to Avoid Fake Work

There is a constant push to plan and project where we will be in the future. Life would be meaningless without some concept of the future driving our action in the present, and most of the work we do would seem meaningless if we didn't think there was a possibility of a lucrative future.

However, if our plans and projections are ill-formed, are unrealistic, or don't take into consideration the needs of the entire company, they can quickly spawn a fresh cycle of fake work. Plans can become a compromised version of reality that quickly takes over in most people's minds, and plans don't contain any actual, guaranteed truths about what will actually happen. The following story illustrates the danger of not focusing work on the present that will help you reach your future goals.

STRATEGY WITHOUT EXECUTION

Russell, the director of a sales team for a multinational high-tech company, was taught in a seminar that if his team was to be successful and execute its work most effectively, it must develop a team strategy and associated strategic goals. Russell set aside two days at a resort in Dubai for his team to determine what its strategy should be and what sales goals the team should attain during the next six months. The team created its strategy by the book; everything was in accordance with sound practices in strategic development. A week after the team returned to their offices, Russell distributed the strategy to all team members, confident and excited with the prospect of success.

At the end of the six-month period, Russell compared the team's performance with the sales goals they had set in Dubai. Not one of the five sales goals had been met. In fact, the team's numbers were hardly better than they were for the previous six months. Russell was mystified as he realized that just setting goals doesn't mean people will be able to achieve them. His team's strategy was sound, but his team's execution was weak.

Russell showed the results to his friend Alex, the vice president of sales. Russell explained that he had used the team to develop sales goals and that he had shared the goals with all team members, yet for some reason they were not executing the strategy. Russell thought that maybe he had the wrong members on his team bus. "What's wrong with these people?" Russell asked Alex.

Alex looked Russell in the eye and asked, "What did you do to get your people to complete the team's sales goals?" Russell responded, "I let them help develop the goals, we printed the goals on cards, and we had a special meeting to review the sales goals."

"But, Russell," Alex replied, "setting goals is just part of the process. How did you help improve your team's execution?"

Alex continued, "Russell, you have good people, but they will not attain the team's sales goals unless you help them understand what they need to do, help them review the work they are currently doing, and hold them accountable for specific tasks. You have good people, a good team strategy, but the team is doing the same work they have always done, work that is not focused on the team's new strategic goals."

Planning and setting goals are important, but without execution you won't get results. If you're not doing work that's real and in line with your goals, you risk sinking into a fake-work trap.

When you get so caught up in your plans for the future that you neglect the present, you risk displacing real work with a goal or target for future work. And planning work can be a particularly invasive form of fake work because it looks and feels so productive. Remember that plans, while useful if based in reality, are no guarantee that actual work will happen. When plans are good, they will help you ensure that real work will be done; when plans are bad, they can become a substitute for actual effort.

Step 4. Realize That Grasping Reality Drives Real Work

Often, people hope that their fake work will become real. This inappropriate hope generates much fake work and wastes valuable energy. Consider the late Admiral Jim Stockdale, as presented by Jim Collins,[1] who, against all odds, survived for eight years in a Vietnamese POW camp. In describing his ordeal, Stockdale recounted how the people least likely to survive the camps were the utter pessimists and the devout optimists. During his imprisonment, Stockdale remained hopeful that he would get out, but he never let hope compromise his ability to deal with the current realities he had to face—torture, humiliation, and isolation. He never set unrealistic deadlines for his release, and he made every day count by focusing on the few things he could control that would have the greatest impact on the men he commanded in the camps.

Stockdale is a brilliant paradigm of reality-based hope, and he's been credited by knowledgeable thinkers like Jim Collins as a true role model in modern organizational development. Stockdale showed a healthy, confident hope that was grounded in reality because he based his expectations and plans on what was actually happening, not what he wanted to be happening.

Hope is not a plan, but without hope, there's no reason to plan at all. Hope is a vital resource in any healthy organization—it provides the impetus for people to do real work, plan for a successful future, and thrive in an organization even during economic downturns. However, *we must base our hopes on reality.* This means that if you're tasked to redesign a combustion engine to run as a hybrid, accept the challenge, but don't disregard the fact that electricity costs are steadily increasing. Or if you're asked to increase your company's sales in the technology sector for the next three quarters, go for it, but be sure to check with the manufacturing department to make sure it can handle the additional load and facilities needed for this kind of growth.

---

1 Jim Collins, *Good to Great* (New York: Harper Business, 2001), 83–87.

The following story illustrates the importance of keeping work and hope based in reality.

Jeremy's Sales Leads

Jeremy, a small business owner, provides marketing services to many local and national businesses. Jeremy was very concerned that his salespeople didn't have the skills to close sales. He had provided his salespeople with a "hot list" of potential clients that he'd compiled over the years, but his people weren't closing deals with anyone on the list of contacts. Jeremy asked us to help him solve the problem. He gave us permission to interview the sales representatives regarding their overall work, and he specifically wanted us to find out the reasons they weren't locking in clients on the "hot list."

The salespeople had all worked for many years in sales, and many had sold the company's products and services for a long time. They were generally very enthusiastic about the company and the products they were selling.

When we asked the team about Jeremy's list, all team members responded similarly. "Jeremy's leads are all at least two years old and most of his contacts are gone. The companies had already purchased our products and wouldn't need to purchase them again for a very long time, and they'd told Jeremy to call back in four or five years. But after five years, many of the companies are either out of business or simply no longer interested. This isn't a hot list, it's a hope list or a morgue list." But the sales team was too nervous to challenge Jeremy and his list.

Our report to Jeremy was brief. We simply let him know the perceptions of the sales team regarding the list. Jeremy was not happy to get the information, but he conceded that the list was really an old "hope list" and no longer based in reality. We suggested that the list was a great producer of fake work, as it was not based in reality, and he grudgingly agreed.

Be real with employees and clients when you're making assumptions about what they need and want, or when you think you know what they're thinking. Clarify the situation, don't be afraid that the effort you're extending to clarify assumptions will be wasted or won't be validated by the employee, and don't be afraid that the employee won't like what you have to offer. If you employ too much hope just because you don't like feeling that you can't control your own future, it still doesn't change anything: Reality is indifferent to your own needs and agenda. Rather than hoping for a better future, hoping for a better pipeline, or hoping for a spike of fourth-quarter sales, you should look at what you have under your control right now and assess how far your current situation is from where you'd like to be. If you have an accurate view of reality, you must then follow your intention to act on a set of facts in a way that you believe will bring about a better future and allow you to do real work.

A Roadmap for Action

- Think through all the activities you do in a given day. How many of them are real? How many of them are fake?

- Why do you do fake work? Whose fault is it—yours, your team's, your supervisor's, your manager's, or your organization's?

- If your work tasks are not real, do you have a plan or an idea to make them real or more closely aligned to your organization's top priorities?

- Whom would you need to talk to in order to make the work you do more real?

- Don't call a meeting or schedule a conference call without clear purpose and clear outputs.

- Don't revise a document that has already been revised if you're not adding value.

- Ask for action items at the end of every meeting and then cut all the ones that would cause fake work.

PATH 2
Escape from Your World of Fake Work

The difference between what we do and what we are capable of doing would suffice to solve most of the world's problems.

—*Mahatma Gandhi*

NOW THAT YOU'VE begun to see how much fake work you do, you need to learn to be flexible and open to new ways of thinking so that you can learn to extricate yourself from fake work. Part of the problem with fake work is that it has become so entrenched in our workplaces that it just seems normal and acceptable. But by thinking differently about what it is you do and how you do it, you can begin to make the shift from fake to real work. The following steps will help you do this:

Step 1: Confront assumptions that promote fake work.
Step 2: Switch from fake work to real work.
Step 3: Be highly flexible.
Step 4: Alert others to fake work.

In our daily work lives we often do fake work that has become so institutionalized by our company that neither we nor the company realizes that it's fake work. We recently heard a story about a very well-known service company that illustrates this situation:

FREEDOM AND FAKE WORK

Sean is a senior manager for a fast-growing service company who was tasked to manage, develop, and expand a new international division over the course of two years.

The company is very team-oriented and operates as a type of open democracy. This is great in theory, but it means that everyone is invited to discuss any issue at any time. The approach has its benefits, but no change is made without open-ended, invite-the-world meetings where idle chit chat is the common denominator. Meetings never end with decisions being made, action plans being put in place, or assignments being given. Employees meet in halls, in offices, in conference rooms, and in the cafeteria to discuss what should happen, but nothing comes about from the discussions. But the employees are happy and feel they are helping the company move forward.

Sean was caught in this culture. After six months of discussions regarding the new international division and how it should move forward, no decisions had been made. Sean's employees enjoyed participating in discussions, but Sean was totally frustrated because he was not even close to meeting his goal to open a hundred new offices.

He went to the CEO, who congratulated him for including his people in the discussions about the international division and told him to keep up the good work. The praise was nice, but what Sean really needed was some backup. Frustrated, finally he decided to push forward and make decisions, action plans, and work assignments on his own. When he tried to do this, however, he was told he needed to spend more time discussing before making decisions. Nine months into this process, Sean submitted his resignation to the CEO. He told the CEO that the company was so open it could not make decisions, and he felt he was wasting time talking but not getting anything done. The CEO appreciated Sean's honesty and drive and tried to get him to stay with the company, but it was too late.

Although Sean had been sick of all the discussions and the lack of progress at the company, it wasn't because these discussions were mostly fake work. Instead, he was exasperated with his own lack of progress and attempted to steamroll his way toward his goal rather than eliminating the fake work that was keeping him back.

The situation described in Sean's story is a relatively common manifestation of fake work. Companies must support their employees and managers must interact with them and use their feedback. At some point, managers must be able to move forward with decisions and plans.

Clearly, Sean's people spent too much time in official interdepartmental meetings discussing and not deciding, and they spent too much time in informal meetings discussing and not acting. They were engaged in fake work, and they did not know it.

What to Know About Path 2

Once You've Seen Fake Work, You Must Escape It

Almost everyone has an instant epiphany when grasping the idea of fake work. It's intuitively compelling, and it deeply resonates with many experiences we've had in our personal and professional lives. And it doesn't take long before we begin to see fake work almost everywhere and in every aspect of our lives.

We see it in the irrelevant meetings we're asked to plan, in the overly cheerful way we celebrate so many birthdays at work, and in the special—but meaningless—projects we are assigned or assign others. We might even get caught up in pointing out the fakeness of everyone we see around us—how the director flits from meeting to meeting without getting anything done, how the marketing department never quite manages to put together an interesting set of materials we can use, or how our assistant is always responding to e-mails but doesn't finish putting together next week's schedule.

It's easy to catch the early zeal against fake work and be out-raged at what you see going on around you. It's like a religious con-version has just struck, and now you've got to go raise the tent and begin converting people like mad. But before you start preaching to the masses, it's important to understand how you can go about changing a fundamental work practice, especially when much of your life may be organized around the support, maintenance, and reproduction of fake work. So where do you begin?

Realize That Change from Fake to Real Work Begins with You

You begin with yourself. You must understand that you *can* make a difference in the fight against fake work. You must rethink the way you see yourself, the people around you, and the world in which you work. You must visualize how work could be more real, and not let your current reality hinder your intent to reduce fake work.

Take note: This doesn't mean thinking differently just to be perverse. It's not about bucking the norm just because you can; instead, it's about cultivating an ability to re-imagine the norm be-cause you perceive something is wrong or fake. You need to under-stand how the world of fake work is formed by and dependent upon habits, processes, systems, and structures. Over time in many companies, these have become institutionalized and rigid to the point where they no longer represent real work. They were created by people and, to a real extent, they're maintained by all of us who buy into them and continue to sleepwalk through our workday not questioning the way things are done, not seeing what's really hap-pening, or not wanting to rock the boat. So we go along and con-tinue to do fake work.

This is a call to shake things up and rattle these calcified and stubborn fake-work practices. You can change these time- and effort-wasting systems if you can change the way you think about them and about yourself.

The rules of work were not written in stone, dictated from a burning bush, or found etched on golden plates. They are consensual and mutual habits that we continue to propagate every time we enter and engage in the workplace. Every moment we are at work, we have the inherent capacity to change and reshape our relationship to our job by thinking about things differently.

So what are some actions you can take to keep from accepting fake work? What are some steps you can take to start thinking differently?

Steps to Move Down Path 2

Step 1: Confront Assumptions That Promote Fake Work

It's easy to see how new managers and corporate leaders can shake things up and quickly reduce fake work, but what if you work in a stable environment that you think might not be living up to its and its people's best abilities? Stability often leads to a false assumption that all is well and that the work you are doing is completely real.

The following story was told by Marcie, a project manager for a large research department of a multinational company. It points out that how you perceive your work is often incorrect.

WHO'S DOING MY RESEARCH?

I run research projects on coloring and additive formulas, and I have been promoted several times because of my strong work performance. The projects my team and I tackle are not easy, and we work long and hard to complete them on time. Usually, we are responding to an urgent request from a distributor somewhere in the world who has some demand or change needed in their market. So, getting the baseline information and getting our process started can be frustrating and is sometimes overwhelming.

We are always struggling with deadlines and budgets and pressure from the top, but that has been where I've shone— that is, until I came head-to-head with an additive and coloring project for a European client that was burning me and my team out. We kept running into all kinds of problems. And I could see that it was going to sink us.

At one point, I started looking through all the other research that had been done in this field of study. This was a painful process because we weren't good about project documentation or archiving systems, and it took so much time to find any helpful information that I wasn't sure if my effort actually helped.

I went back to Europe to do some additional interviewing with the client and ensure that we understood the problem. While I was there, I learned nothing earthshaking, but I did run into Garrett, a fellow project manager. He was working on a similar project, and because we hardly ever saw each other, we decided to have dinner together.

We agreed not to talk about work, but about midway through dinner he started asking me questions about how I ran projects, since my reputation was so good. I was trying not to show how vulnerable I was feeling and how the current project was going to miss deadlines, budgets, and expectations. But the more he asked, the more phony I felt—and I finally admitted that I didn't feel like a role model at that point.

That opened a conversation that I will never forget. I told him about my project and about all the problems we were running into. Suddenly he interrupted me and said, "Wait a minute, your worries are over. My team has already done most of that research." I couldn't believe my good luck.

Over the next few hours, we discovered much more than just the sad reality of an information gap. We talked about the other project teams and realized that we were all working alone, as if we were distinct little company city-states. Back from Europe, Garrett and I then decided to do something. We went to the VP of research and asked him if he was aware of this issue. He admitted that he knew of several instances where our project work was repetitive, but he was unsure how to solve the problem given our demanding schedule, and he seemed content that we were each getting our research done and solving our clients' problems. We asked for and received permission to do an internal assessment, and we brought in some outside help to investigate the problem and to recommend changes.

Through our assessment we learned that 25 percent of our project time was wasted on doing baseline research that had been done before—in many cases, several times before. To put that in perspective, our average research project budget was just over $135,000, so we could estimate that about $34,000 was wasted on every project. We did more than 125 projects each year; therefore, about $4.25 million each year was wasted on duplicated research. And that doesn't count the real costs that aren't calculated into any project budget, like turnover rates—our turnover was much higher than that of similar businesses. The deeper the consultants looked, the uglier it got.

At first I felt proud that Garrett and I had opened up the can of worms, but then I started to feel awful. I realized that the weekends I'd spent working could have been spent with my husband and kids. My team members had sacrificed family events and vacations to help me fulfill our project expectations. Plus, I had been totally disconnected from my real team. I'd thought my team was the people who were put on my projects, but it was actually a team of project managers, leaders, and research managers all throughout the company who could have been collaborating and sharing information with me.

Finally, I found out that the company was investigating our research group because our costs were higher and our outputs lower than our company's other facilities. They were considering closing us down. I realized that for years I had been praised, rewarded, and allowed to believe that I was doing great work in the face of serious concerns that could have resulted in the loss of my job and those of most of the researchers I had worked with for years. The realization was devastating. Along with Garrett and other colleagues we made dramatic changes in project management, knowledge management, and other processes and systems that turned things around.

This story is, unfortunately, common in so many companies. Marcie, Garrett, and their teams of researchers weren't avoiding hard work. They were committed, dedicated, and professional. But the fact is, they were doing fake work, and it almost cost them their jobs. Fortunately, Marcie realized that new thinking, relationship-building, and efforts to problem-solve with management could stop the fake-work flow before it was too late.

Don't let your assumptions keep you from discovering the fake work you do. Be aware of how information is shared in your organization, and be on the lookout for ways to streamline the work process and stay connected with other teams within your company that could be helpful to you. Don't assume that your tasks are unique or that your company is set up in the most efficient way.

Step 2: Switch from Fake Work to Real Work

The world of work is changing as we speak. With the onset of knowledge-based work brought on by the technical and computer revolution, we are in a period of major transition from blue-collar, manufacturing work, in which teams were commonly set up in a hierarchical, militaristic model, into white-collar, information-based work, where teams are set up horizontally and flexibly.

But for many of us, while history has moved forward, we're still operating in a set of older, rigid ideas about work. In the new era, the very idea of what constitutes work is hard to define. And the old ways of structuring manufacturing work often don't work with knowledge- or information-based work. In manufacturing, the amount of real work you're doing is usually obvious. But in many service-oriented industries, it's often difficult to tell if responding to an e-mail or attending a meeting or doing research constitutes real work. You might be working on the most mission-critical initiatives for your company, but from the outside, no one would be able to tell you apart from the guy who is e-mailing his girlfriend.

Because we have inherited the old-model idea that equates real work with the turnout of a product—a car, a widget, a computer chip—it's often difficult to value work that has few tangible outcomes. The result: Many people have made their work seem more real by trying to introduce products—even unnecessary ones—in projects, meetings, and deliverables. And that is fake work.

Even when the work produced is very tangible, it can still amount to fake work if what's produced is not what's needed—especially if it prevents something that *is* needed from being done. Here's an example that might strike a chord with you:

WAXING AND FAKE WORK

Andy was head of the custodial team for a large regional bank. His assignment was to keep the bank's branches and the surrounding grounds clean, appealing, and customer-friendly. Andy's team worked hard—in fact, they complained of being overworked—but the custodians worked far too much on some tasks while neglecting others. For example, they waxed all the floors three times a week, but often didn't trim the shrubs or restock the restrooms.

Eventually, Andy's boss called him in and complained about the condition of the grounds and the lack of paper towels. Andy was furious. He told his boss that he was concerned about making his staff work even harder.

Andy and his boss met a week later and his boss pointed out that waxing the floors three times a week was unnecessary. If Andy would cut the waxing back to once a week, his team would have plenty of time for the other work.

Andy was incensed by this discussion and his boss's unwillingness to see how hard his employees worked. Therefore, he submitted his resignation on the spot. The problem was, Andy was unwilling to change his routine and rethink the way he and his team did their work.

Like Andy, who refused to acknowledge that all that excessive floor-waxing was fake work that prevented real work, all of us sometimes need to rethink the value of the tasks we do. Are we doing fake work that could be eliminated with small changes in our specific work assignments? To eliminate fake work, you must constantly question the structure of work, how you fit into it, and how you might go about changing it for the better.

Too many people and companies have a great reservoir of untapped ability because they operate in inflexible situations that, inevitably, generate work that's outmoded and unproductive. And this rigidity has limited our growth and progress as individuals because we haven't been allowed to change things around or conceptualize work in a different, valuable, or more contemporary way.

Step 3: Be Highly Flexible

If you learn to see your work differently, change will gradually happen as you dip your toes into the water of what's real and right. Change doesn't happen overnight, but we've seen miraculous strides made by people who are brave enough to be flexible.

But change is hard for some people. Even though you may be waking up to the idea of fake work, some may balk at the idea of change and become rigid and unyielding unless that change is directed at someone else. As Peter M. Senge put it in *The Fifth Discipline*, "People don't resist change, they resist being changed." And we've seen business revolutions where change was brutally and inefficiently forced on many people to no great end. We think that's a hopelessly ineffective way to go about making changes in an organization.

You need to practice being flexible and learn how to open your mind over an extended period of time in a conscious way. Take the example of Stan, a member of an engineering design team for a large manufacturing company:

STAN RISES TO THE TOP

As an engineer, Stan was a great member of the team who always got his work done on time, had lots of ideas to contribute about streamlining the design process, and was responsible for producing some of the most innovative retooling his team did. But as good as Stan was technically, he was continually passed up for leadership positions because he was perceived as having low self-esteem, a trait that might hamper his ability to be an effective leader. Stan's supervisors jumped to this conclusion for a variety of reasons—he had a low management performance score, and he'd missed an important customer meeting two years ago, among other little reasons—and once that perception was put into place, no one ever questioned it. They basically saw Stan as a specialist and individual contributor with no leadership expertise.

During a corporate restructuring initiative, Stan's direct supervisor was promoted to a different unit in the organization, and his new supervisor was almost immediately ordered to reduce staff by 15 percent before the end of the fourth quarter. Stan's team leader and three others got laid off, and Stan was promoted to team leader. Stan had never been a manager and he had to learn from scratch how to lead.

His team had always met minimal expectations but had never stood out, but Stan started redesigning some of their larger processes based on ideas he'd come up with over the years but never dared to suggest they implement. His re-engineering of the system sped up his team's timeline for introducing designs on the manufacturing line and significantly reduced the number of steps in the manufacturing process. Stan's work helped the team reach a previously unknown level of success. Other team leaders were impressed by Stan's systematized design process and his elimination of time-wasting processes. They started watching Stan to see why he was so successful.

After about three months, Stan started to hold informal team leader meetings where he exchanged reengineering information and ideas on how to do away with pointless exercises. His supervisor was pleased and recommended him for further promotion: she felt that Stan had been a hidden superstar in a calcified, rigid workplace that couldn't wake up to see his actual talents.

Stan succeeded by being flexible, capable of fostering change, and by being an enemy to fake work. He was able to leverage his skill and move up the corporate ladder by being able to think differently about what he could do. Stan knew he had good technical design ability, but he didn't believe that he had good management skills because he'd never been able to test them. When his situation changed, he suddenly rose to the occasion and used his untapped abilities to reshape the manufacturing process and eliminate steps that weren't necessary.

Being able to think differently is the key to retaining flexibility. When Stan got the chance, he functioned flexibly and created a new process that reduced fake work and increased productivity—to everyone's benefit.

Step 4: Alert Others to Fake Work

One of the key reasons some of us continue to do fake work is that although we recognize fake work, we don't know how to share that realization with others, especially our bosses. We sometimes assume that our bosses and our colleagues might think we are being silly if we discuss fake work. So we continue on doing work that is of no value and that does not further our company's efforts. This is unacceptable, and here's an example of why:

FAKE BRAKE PADS

Sarah works for a bicycle manufacturing company. She has spent the past six months on a project developing brake pads for a certain model of bicycle, even though she and many of the people on her team know that model will be discontinued in a few months. Still, no one says anything to management because the workers fear they might lose their jobs if the company discontinues the brake project. So Sarah's team comes to work every day and develops a brake pad that will never be used. The team members know they are doing fake work. They are unhappy but afraid to do anything differently. They keep doing fake work and the project does nothing but cost the company money.

Sarah had contemplated talking to her boss about the situation, but she is fearful of losing her job and concerned that her boss will get upset with her. So she goes to work each day and creates a brake pad that will never exist.

This situation may sound unbelievably ridiculous, but it is surprisingly common in the corporations that we visit. People are doing fake work and they know it, but no one seems to want to tell management about it, or to turn it into meaningful and real work. Why? Usually the reasons are similar to Sarah's team's, but more complicated. Perhaps one of the following is a reason you haven't spoken up yet:

Reasons for Not Blowing the Whistle on Others About Fake Work

- *Worry about losing your job.* In these days of downsizing and distrust toward leadership, it is no wonder that employees are often fearful about losing their jobs. Employees doing fake work might fear that if they eliminate the fake work by blowing the whistle on themselves, they will no longer have a purpose in the organization. This is likely the largest cause of fake work in many organizations—If I don't do my fake work, what will I do?

- *Worry that others could lose their jobs.* Just as employees don't want to endanger their own jobs, they also don't want to endanger the jobs of their colleagues. Because of this fear, work teams have even made pacts not to mention to others they are doing fake work.
- *Fear of the boss or other leaders.* Leaders should be doing everything they can to make sure their employees are not doing fake work, but in many cases leaders simply dole out assignments and are forceful about their expectations that the tasks be completed as told. Employees are often unwilling to challenge the relevance of the tasks, and are often fearful of questioning authority, or specifically, a boss who is intimidating. They don't feel they are in a safe environment for honest input. The boss-employee relationship causes people who are being supervised to want to please the boss and to not reveal what is really happening. Leaders should encourage their direct reports to let them know more than that the job is being completed successfully—specifically, is the job meaningful in terms of the organization's goals?
- *Fear of ruining a leader's pet project.* The more we visit organizations, the more we see leaders who develop projects that they become emotionally attached to but aren't supporting their organization's strategies. This emotional attachment causes leaders to hold on to projects that are obviously fake work to other workers. However, most employees are loath to criticize a pet project of one of their leaders for fear of creating bad blood, or even getting fired.

How to Let Others Know About Fake Work

Employees at all levels must question fake work when they see it. Often it is difficult to overcome the fear associated with revealing what is happening, but it has to be done and there are ways to do so while minimizing the potentially negative consequences. Here's how.

- *Be courageous, and embrace change.* People who are willing to point out fake work and the need for change usually feel secure about their work and their jobs. They are confident in themselves and feel that they are seen as valuable contributing employees. So believe in yourself, and when you discover a fake-work situation, go to your immediate leader and discuss it. If you realize you're doing fake work, you can probably envision a solution, and can play up all the valuable, real work you do (and could be doing more of).

    Don't think too much about your fears; think about being supportive of your company.
- *Be direct, and offer solutions.* When you go to your leader, be direct and get to the point immediately. Describe the fake-work situation you are witnessing and tell the leader how you think it could be changed. Allow the leader time for his or her reactions, then restate your concern, your ideas, and your willingness to help in any way. The key is to describe the problem with a high level of professionalism, sincerity, and concern; if you express your ideas with anger, insensitivity, or arrogance, your leader is far less likely to accept your suggestion.
- *Tell the truth.* When describing the fake-work situation to your leader, tell the truth as you see it. Don't exaggerate or make up stories to strengthen your position.
- *Meet your responsibility.* Meet your responsibility to the company by giving your point of view and describing the fake work as you see it. Whether your leaders do anything about the fake work is up to them, but you will have done your best and met your responsibility to your company.

In sum, part of the problem with fake work is that it has become so entrenched in the workplace that it just seems normal and acceptable. By thinking differently about what fake work is, you can escape from your world of fake work and make the work you do more real and more meaningful for your company.

A Roadmap for Action

- Assess your job and your life thoroughly and get a sense of the difference you feel when doing real work versus fake work.

- List all the things, people, ideas, and structures you take for granted at work.

- List your least flexible points.

- List your most flexible points.

- Describe how you think things could change in your own workplace.

- Describe your fears in discussing the fake work you see in your company.

- Describe your strategy for telling your boss about the fake work you see.

PATH 3

Just Do It! Real Work

Knowing is not enough; we must apply.
Willing is not enough; we must do.

—*Bruce Lee*

PATH 3 IS about putting all the awareness you have gained about fake work in Paths 1 and 2 into action in the workplace. This path stresses that real work exists in a cycle of awareness and focus on key strategic priorities, followed by action. This path encourages you to do real work. In fact, the most important word to keep in mind as you review this chapter is the word *do*, and to that end we provide you with four steps for successfully doing real work:

Step 1: Make the leap to real work.
Step 2: Avoid the disappointing consequences of not doing real work.
Step 3: Align your work tasks with key company priorities.
Step 4: Implement the three-tiered process of analyzing, doing, and adjusting.

Path 3 is important because it is critical for each of us to act now in our jobs and to do real work. We often find ourselves in comfortable positions that encourage us to continue with the status quo, and it just seems easiest not to do anything to reduce fake work. However, the following story about Myrna illustrates the importance of action and doing.

THE SALES DELIVERY LIAISON

After I received my MBA, I went to work for a small communications firm. This was my first relatively high-level position, and I was excited about the pay. I knew I was on my way up the corporate ladder. I was hired to act as the liaison between Sales and Delivery: Both divisions always had inevitable disputes about pricing and timeline, and my job was to mediate their problems and to speed up the sales cycle across the board.

I was the third person to hold this job over the course of fifteen years, and the CEO told me at a cocktail party that he considered it a grooming slot for other, more key positions in the company. It was flattering to have garnered the job, since I had beaten out two or three other people on the company's inside track to get it. I was excited to be there.

I quickly learned, however, that it was basically a management-level position without any real responsibility, and I started asking some pointed questions about what I was supposed to accomplish. The head of sales told me, "You're supposed to convince the delivery people that our prices are too high and schedules are too long for us to sell anything." The head of delivery said just the opposite: "You're supposed to fight for pricing and schedule integrity."

I took my own assessment of the situation and then tried to validate it. I decided to act as my own auditor and started to do some data gathering and cause-effect analysis. I soon realized that my job was really just an excuse for me to create a little empire and that it prevented Sales and Delivery from actually talking to each other in a productive way. In other words, I realized that, structurally, my job consisted of preventing these two groups of people from confronting problems and finding new solutions. No matter how you looked at it, my job was way out of alignment with the critical goals of the company. I was being paid to add a bureaucratic step that actually reduced our productivity.

Clearly, Myrna was caught in a fake-work trap. What may not be as clear is what she could do to escape it. She should start by reviewing this fake-work situation with her boss. And then she should try to bring the heads of sales and delivery together so they could have meaningful discussions about the goals of the company in an effort to find common ground. What she can't do is sit in her position and continue to do fake work.

What to Know About Path 3

Companies Need Good People Who Do Real Work

All the awareness and focus in the world about your problem can't help you if you don't do anything about it. If you don't act, you'll inevitably end up walking around and talking about how things should be done, rather than doing things the way they ought to be done. Be sure to act with personal integrity in a way that rewards both you and your company by being aligned with key company strategies and by eliminating fake work.

Bear in mind that it's not always an easy transition from merely being aware of fake work to actually succeeding in aligning your work tasks to critical strategy. For one thing, fake work might be work that needs to be done, but loses its value in endless deadline shifts, inefficient work processes, and duplication of effort. But the positive consequences of making the leap are huge. Just imagine how it would feel to know that your work on a given day contributed twice as much to your company as it used to.

The following story from Grace, who works for a manufacturing company, will inspire you to look for ways to increase the amount of real work you do and reduce the amount of fakeness, as well as stress, in your life.

WHEN REDUCING WORK RESPONSIBILITIES
INCREASES REAL WORK

As an internal organizational consultant, I got lots of praise for taking on the tough stuff. I was always picking up projects that others didn't want, always in overload, and I seldom said no. I thought that I was making my mark. I had been promoted and received raises, and I felt that I was doing something right.

My boss put me on a project that involved working with business leaders to analyze their measures of success for project work, process analysis, and other initiatives, and then creating an implementation and coaching program to get managers and supervisors on board with the proposed changes.

While I was working on that project, I picked up an orientation project that seemed relatively easy, and I kept the momentum going on both projects.

Then, when one of my colleagues went on maternity leave, I picked up her project on updating our quality control process. So now I was working on three big projects and several small things.

Three months later, Alexandra, my boss, called me into her office. I was expecting to get a pat on the back for keeping all those balls in the air. Instead, Alexandra told me she had heard complaints that important projects were not getting enough attention and were drifting into oblivion. My boss was kind and tried to show appreciation for all my effort and hard work, but she was really telling me that I was trying to handle too many things. I defended myself. I explained how I was covering everything. She stopped me. We discussed the project plans, deadlines, and her concerns about closing out those projects. She acknowledged that I was working hard, but she pointed out that all my deadlines were drawn out because I wasn't targeting the right goals. As much as I hated to admit it, I realized that I had lost my focus in the midst of lots of hard work. I was being snapped back into reality: Alexandra was distinguishing my hard work from the priorities of the business.

We agreed that I needed to hand off the reins for the quality control project and instead serve as a team member (which was hard because I like to manage projects). I put the orientation project on hold until the end of the year. I felt focused and connected for the first time in months. But most importantly, I was at least 50 percent more efficient. I created a real project plan, pulled all my team members together, and finished the measures-of-success project way ahead of the former schedule. The leaders who had complained about my lack of focus suddenly went out of their way to thank me for getting this complicated project off the ground.

It wasn't easy changing the way I work and how I perceived my own prowess. I'd thought I had no limitations. But when I focused my hard work on key priorities and strategies, as well as on getting the right things done—and done quickly—I saw where my real value to the company lay. I felt proud of the new me. And I started sleeping better and feeling stress-free.

Just because Grace had good intentions and was willing to take on every project didn't make her effective. Grace was feeling pressure from her clients, her boss, and herself that all prevented her from being able to focus on what is real. Even if she could have pulled off all the projects somehow, the quality of her work would have been called into question.

It's easy to wrap yourself in cynicism and malign your company for ineptitude or poor systems and processes, but sometimes the problem is your own inability to see how you could best assist your company in reaching its goals. Grace was lucky that her boss helped her regain focus; lots of companies work really hard to attract, retain, and support good people but ultimately fail because they don't tap into the true contribution or value of their individual people.

The Spirit of Real Work

When you choose to become a doer of real work, you effectively move away from the letter of your job and into the spirit. You learn to insert value into each situation by getting outside the regular patterns of expectation set up by your job description, years of experience working in the same place, and "common-sense" kinds of thinking about what needs to get done.

Most of us tend to approach work reactively: We conduct our workday by responding to the things that happen around us rather than proactively applying our work effort to things that matter. Instead of ignoring a phone call from another VP, we pick it up and get carried down a path we haven't chosen for ourselves. Or we attend the board meeting and, surprised, accept an offer to run a major environmental initiative that we didn't know was in the works. In other words, we let the circumstances and accidents of our work life dictate how we act.

To always have the spirit of real work in mind, remember to:

- *Maintain a different orientation to your work.* Constantly look at your job, your tasks, and your routine from different points of view. This will help you see what truly matters.
- *Exercise control and discipline.* Instead of getting blown like a leaf by the wind, exercise discipline to cut through all the waste and focus your limited energy on what truly matters, rather than something irrelevant or fake.
- *Become a doer of real work.* Becoming a doer of real work requires practice, but it's the kind of practice that everyone can get used to, and it doesn't take years to master. Just focus on your company's goals and do what you can to help reach them. Remember that talking isn't doing, and that having an open mind will allow you to devise the best, most efficient solutions.

So how do you become a valued employee and ensure you're a doer of real work? The following four steps will guide you:

Steps to Move Down Path 3

Step 1: Make the Leap to Real Work

Companies need brave people who are willing to make the leap from fake to real work. That leap begins with you. Your company might not be aware the leap even needs to be made, but you can help your coworkers see the light.

Take a look around your company and the other areas of your life and identify people who are effective. We all talk about them, know who they are, and marvel at what they are able to accomplish. They're people who cut to the heart of the matter, stay above the daily trivial distractions, and do great things that are based on prioritized, effective work that's really critical to their companies. They seem to accomplish miracles when all the people around them just seem to do what they need to do to get by.

These self-aware people bring something special to the work environment: an ability to channel their creativity, energy, passion, and insight into doing great work that serves the core of their company. They constantly surprise companies with new ideas, concepts, or even small changes that produce radical results. Their innovations are often so revolutionary and trendsetting that when you look back at the company's history, you can't imagine what it would have been like without them. They are the success stories of every company, and they're the people who get rewarded, promoted, and celebrated. Such people are the employees who make leaps, and by modeling yourself after them you can become a success story as well.

Tracy, the CFO of a young financial consulting company, told us the following story about Amit, a star employee at her company who changed the way Tracy approached her work.

MAKIN' IT HAPPEN

We hired Amit to help us with marketing. We had great services and great people and seemed poised for a launch. Amit created new brochures and mailers and a variety of service-related materials for our salespeople that were all well received and very helpful. Our biggest goal was to increase revenue and, of course, increase sales by getting more leads and connecting with more potential customers.

Amit spent a lot of time with the salespeople and even more with the leadership team. He kept asking what our strategies were. We thought they were clear to all our employees. He was quiet, but he kept hinting that something seemed broken. He took on a new task as analyst. He didn't tell anyone, but I kind of knew he was digging into other things. He started with our sales model and pricing, and he quickly realized that we had a very flawed pricing structure. Basically, we were pricing our consulting days like products—the larger the quantity, the lower the price per unit—so our two-day product cost only slightly less than our three-day product. Amit pointed out that we weren't in the business of selling products; we were selling consulting days. And we were almost giving the third day away free. It seemed so obvious. How had we missed that? Immediately, we changed the pricing model. Overnight our revenue picked up and, over time, rose 17 percent just because of that adjustment.

Next, Amit discovered that we had a thousand leads and a ton of small contracts—some of which were with very small offices within very large corporations. He knew we had an excellent reputation and we could leverage our relationships, so he redesigned our sales model to target the home offices of the small offices that were satisfied with our services. When he brought the plan to me, I created a reward for package deals that expanded our relationship with these big companies to provide services to many more of their offices. Within a few months, we were killing our old sales numbers. All the salespeople were tripling their dollars per sale, and all of them were working with fewer customers but giving them more time and attention and getting great results. It was simple and it was genius.

Amit went from creating leaflets to send out to people who didn't need us or know us to focusing on real business. He analyzed our company and figured out what our real strategies needed to be. Then he jumped into the work that we needed done—not what we had asked him to do. He changed our business and our results in less than nine months.

"Do it" people like Amit combine bravery, focus, and integrity without becoming overly involved in their own personal agendas. Instead of thinking about their own importance, they make even the smallest task important because they act with great precision and creativity. They do a great job because they are fundamentally committed to doing work that's real and right. And they understand the difference between simple tasks and *critical tasks* that drive a company's fundamental purpose.

Not everyone has the intelligence and bravery to look at a task that's been assigned by a boss and put it at the bottom of his work pile, and know that's the right thing to do for the company. In fact, our research shows that most people are off track almost 50 percent of the time, and they spend their days languishing in unimportant, irrelevant tasks. Most of these folks don't realize that if you and your team are just slightly out of alignment, you can effectively miss the mark altogether. Be brave enough to transform both your own work situation and your company by focusing on real work and doing it in the most creative, innovative, and precise ways that you can.

Step 2: Avoid the Disappointing Consequences of Not Doing Real Work

The following story illustrates the painful consequences Lindsay experienced while working on a "hot" project.

MARKETING THE VOID

My manager put me on a hot project, initiated by our leadership team, that required me to research potential markets for some new pharma-technology products. The project lasted for more than eleven months and involved over fifty people, seven full time, plus outside consulting support. The costs were enormous. The project was a killer—long nights and weekends. We worked hard and then harder to make sense out of the project, generally with no clear direction from the ones who had initiated it. Finally, in spite of the clueless sponsor's problems that derive from working with such a huge group of contributors, I pulled together the report and closed the project. Our report was over 350 pages.

We waited, then pushed to get an audience with Marketing Leadership and other sponsors to present the report and our findings. But we were never able to arrange it. Finally we bound the report and distributed it to all of them and to others we were told were waiting for it.

We never presented our findings in person to anyone. And we never got any feedback—in fact, we have reason to believe that no one ever read the findings. When a couple of our team members brought this up to leaders and managers, their responses implied that they hadn't given our efforts an ounce of attention. The report seemed to have dropped off the earth. We later discovered that a leader in another group had brought in a couple of specialists who had studied the same issue and given them what the sponsors had thought they needed.

A few months after the project had been completed, the company did some downsizing. Four of the seven full-timers from my team were fired, including me. Some of us were told we were just part of the cut, but my manager told me the truth—perhaps because he was leaving the company and felt he had nothing to lose: I was cut because I had been on an expensive project that nobody gave a darn about. I have never felt more devalued. And my manager was leaving because he was on the chopping block for being a part of spending a fortune on an empty project.

The most devastating part of this story is that early on, I had deep suspicions that the project was not what it was

trumped up to be. I saw lots of signs that I ignored. I am an excellent project leader who ignored the warnings to get a feather
in my cap: bad assumptions, ignored intuitions, too few questions, and not nearly enough challenge to our key stakeholders.
I hadn't bothered to ask if there was an easier route. I could
have been a hero. Instead I was fired.

You might be able to relate to such a situation, or perhaps you
can only imagine what pain would come from losing your job after
doing such hard work, exhibiting such devotion, and putting forth
such remarkable effort. This project was doomed by fake work and
propagators of fake work who took no responsibility for their part
in it. Lindsay's confessional revealed that she knew that she not
only had to recognize and fight against fake work but also had to
be doing real work, work that made a difference to the company.
But she ignored her instincts and suffered the consequences.

Failing to do real work is perhaps even more dangerous than
failing to avoid fake work. The risks include:

- *You will end up inadvertently committed to the wrong life path
  or job.* You may or may not be competent at what you do, but
  you will spend most of the day justifying why you decide to do
  one thing rather than another. Your work will likely meet with
  mediocre results, and you will feel that most of what you do
  doesn't amount to much or contribute anything.
- *You will do fake work just to survive.* You'll know that your work
  doesn't contribute anything, but you won't have the confidence
  to stand up and stop doing it. You will feel desperate and anx-
  ious and you won't want to read the writing on the wall when
  your company starts to downsize, but you'll figure it's better to
  look busy while doing fake work than to look for a way out of
  your fake-work trap.
- *Fake work will eventually catch up to you.* In other cases, you
  may like what you do, and you may really think you're making
  a difference. But you'll find that you've put your head in the
  sand about the work you do and the effect it has on the people

around you. If you haven't made sure that the work you're doing is real and aligned, it may well be creating further fake work that might come back to haunt you.

- *You might discover too late that you are doing work you don't like or doing your real work badly.* You'll find that you don't like what you are actually supposed to be doing, and it will show. Over the course of your career, the effects of this personal misalignment can be debilitating. You'll be accused of having a bad attitude and being a slacker. You'll also be compromised in terms of your professional development because you'll lack the basic energy and creativity that you need to do a good job.
- *Your company won't see you as valuable.* You'll be asked to do lots of things that no one cares about. Other people's expectations of you will be lower than they ought to be, and you'll feel it. You'll experience constant setbacks and won't be able to rise through the company in a way commensurate with your talent, experience, and education.
- *You'll have very little influence.* Your personal power will be constrained within your company. People won't act on your suggestions because they know that your work doesn't amount to much of anything or affect anything real. People will rely on you to do things for them, but you will rarely be able to get other people to do things for you.

Real work is dynamic and happens in a constant cycle of doing and aligning. Make sure that you are doing real work and then keep on doing it.

Step 3: Align Your Work Tasks with Key Company Priorities

This step is simple once you train yourself to be mindful—rather than robotic—at work. Examine your work tasks, align them to key company strategies, perform them, and then continue to check that they're in exact alignment with your company's key priorities. Muster the courage to stop doing something you've been doing for a long time when you find out it's not contributing anything to your company's goals, and when necessary, step outside the bounds of your job description and argue that things should be done differently or that company strategy should be changed because it's not moving things forward. Above all, pay attention to what you are doing and make sure what you are doing is helping your company achieve its goals.

Lots of people squander their effort with long to-do lists that are chock-full of busywork. Watch out for tasks that deflect energy from real work that can make a real difference.

The following story illustrates what happens when your daily work tasks are not aligned with your organization's priorities.

THE TRASH CAN REPORT

Roland, a consultant, was working with a company on an internal systems review as the company prepared to install a new manufacturing system. As part of the review, Roland interviewed the marketing manager. She told him that, several years earlier, she had anticipated that the president might someday ask for a particular report.

So, for years, she had three staff people spend about three days each compiling the report at the end of each month and sending him a copy. This report sounded to Roland like an activity that could easily be automated. He checked with the president's office to see how the report was used.

Roland learned that the report wasn't being used at all. In fact, the president's secretary threw the report into the trash each month as soon as it arrived. Apparently the president looked at it when it was first sent, years ago, and then told the secretary he didn't need to see it ever again.

Rather than telling the marketing manager not to produce the report, the secretary simply intercepted it each month and threw it away. Roland calculated that the company had wasted about two years' worth of work generating a report that went straight into the trash.

Situations like the one Roland discovered are amazingly common. Critical work tasks don't tend to be evaluated very often, so as needs and priorities change, many of these tasks are no longer aligned with company needs. And so they become fake work, not real work. If you ensure that the work you're doing really benefits your company, you'll enjoy the success and satisfaction of real work.

Step 4: Implement the Three-Tier Real-Work Process: Analyzing, Doing, and Adjusting

The three-tier real-work process is modeled on the careful, precise procedures that an internal auditor undertakes. Despite the stereotype of auditors as niggling bureaucrats who are trapped in financial details and never see the big picture, internal auditors actually (or at least should) act as business partners, problem solvers, consultants, even coaches. They have the potential to collaborate with individual teams, divisions, or business units to articulate an innovative vision of the problem at hand and to recommend a solution. Because the auditing process breaks down tasks step by step and determines the value of each step, it's a great way for you to figure out exactly what work you do is valuable to the company— and what is not. It also provides a structure that specifies the value of every critical work step. The three tiers of the real-work auditing process are:

1. *Analyzing your work.* Analyze the task at hand. How important is it? Does it relate to key company strategies? Should you be doing it? If so, what exactly should you do?
2. *Doing real work.* Do the work you're supposed to do. It sounds obvious, but far too many people don't get around to accomplishing their most important tasks because they waste their time with other items on their to-do list.
3. *Evaluating and adjusting your performance.* Measure the results of the work you do against company standards, industry benchmarks, or relevant survey instruments. If your situation does

not have such formal data, ask the opinion of your colleagues or your supervisor. How does your work stack up? Does it accomplish what is needed? Is it fake work? Adjust your work according to the feedback you receive.

The process is simple. However, it's remarkable how few people put it into practice. Often, people just set about doing the tasks they're given without ever stopping to question why they are doing them, how they will contribute to company success, or whether they actually succeeded at what they were asked to do. Here is a breakdown of each of the three tiers:

Tier 1: Analyzing Your Work

Often someone will immerse himself in a task without analyzing what that task will achieve, and whether it's being done in the most sensible way. Consider the example of David, a PR director:

WASTED BRANDING

David is accosted in the parking lot by his friend Liz, the director of branding. Liz tells David that a new water desalinization machine will be rolling out in the next month. Excited, David starts a major initiative in his department to work up the PR pitch before the big internal announcement he expects to take place next week.

After three weeks, David still hasn't heard about any announcements, but he keeps his people plugging away at prototypes for the marketing plan. He contacts Product Development and asks for some basic information about the new equipment, but he never receives any scheduling or rollout information. By the fourth week, David gets suspicious and checks in with the VP of product development—and finally hears that the new machine is not working properly and that it will be at least six months before the problem can be worked out. Only then does David realize that he and his staff have wasted four weeks of hard work—and put off several important projects—because he never bothered to verify some news he heard one day in a parking lot.

David had reacted to somebody else's reality and never bothered to check if it matched the company's reality as a whole. He should have analyzed the basic facts at hand before he began his work. Specifically, David should have taken Liz's tidbit of information and immediately verified it with the VP of product development.

David showed a lot of initiative, creativity, and spunk in his reaction to Liz's information—he heard news he thought was true and acted on it decisively—and he didn't wait to be told what to do. Making bold, decisive, or creative moves can add tremendous value to your company—but not if they're based on bad information or are poorly thought out. Because David reacted blindly to the situation instead of analyzing what needed to be done, he ended up doing a ton of fake work, and put off doing real work as well.

Tier 2: Doing Real Work

Once you've analyzed your task and begun your work, you still risk falling back into the fake-work trap if you fail to recognize your priorities. Consider Amadi, an account rep for three high-profile clients and a dozen mid- to low-level clients in the advertising industry.

HIGH-PROFILE VS. LOW-PROFILE CLIENTS

Amadi is an overachiever whose view of her abilities is determined by the number of important clients or projects she works with. She likes to be assigned to task forces, and she's always running off to power lunches or schlepping her clients to Broadway shows to network and impress. She thinks she's got her finger on the pulse of the company and that she's positioned to succeed as she secures more and more important clients.

While Amadi spends enormous amounts of time cultivating her top three accounts, she practically ignores her mid- to low-level clients, whose total account value exceeds the combined value of two of her top three accounts. Amadi knows she needs to pay more attention to them, but she is frequently interrupted by cell phone calls, e-mail queries, and questions from staff assistants regarding the top three clients. She knows things are falling through the cracks, but she also knows that her company really values its high-profile clients. Amadi feels she could lose one or two low-profile clients without raising anyone's eyebrows, but if her bosses receive one negative report about her from a major client, it could well cost her her job. And so, Amadi's top clients suck up more than 80 percent of her time and effort, even though they don't account for anywhere near 80 percent of her accounts' revenue.

Amadi fails to do what's needed in either Tier 1 or Tier 2. She never analyzes what each client means to her bottom line or how she should apportion her time among them. Amadi also fails in Tier 2—she doesn't do the work she really should be doing. Instead, she does the work that makes her seem the busiest and gets her positive reviews from her three pampered clients while the rest suffer.

If Amadi learned to follow the Three-Tier Real-Work Process, she'd learn that she usually functions in a reactive mode: She waits for her clients to call and demand something. Likewise, she waits until her staff apprises her of the current batch of tickets, perks, and swag that is available for her use. In a nutshell, Amadi is always at the mercy of people who call her, interrupt her, or furnish her with the things she needs for her clients, and she never feels she gets ahead of the game. And because she attaches so much importance to *looking* and *feeling* busy, Amadi has very little motivation to change.

The Three-Tier Real-Work Process could help Amadi by teaching her to focus her time on the client issues that matter—not the real or fake emergencies, or the opportunities to schmooze.

Tier 3: Evaluating and Adjusting Your Performance

As much as we all love to judge others' performance, we rarely remember to collect data on our own performance. That's a big mistake. However, self-evaluation is a critical step in every work project because it lets us compare what we actually do versus what we are expected to do and what really needs to get done. In turn, you can adjust your performance to ensure that your work is better aligned with key company priorities.

Evaluation is, in one sense, the ultimate way to guarantee that real work is done because it forces you to measure your effort in terms of actual effect. If your work is misaligned or fake, your evaluation will register red flags in the form of observations like "The project seemed off track before it even started," "I don't really know what this is supposed to accomplish," or "I'm not really sure if this made a difference to the overall picture."

Consider Abraham's story of a design team that was asked to update a ten-year-old design for a portable generator.

THE PORTABLE POWER GENERATOR

The generator was an industry classic and was sold in almost every hunting or outdoor sporting goods store. It ran off two large car batteries that simultaneously charged one while using the other. And it could be patched into a car battery for a quick start. Campers, hunters, and RV users loved it because it was priced low and would run for years without needing a new battery.

Because the company sold a lot of its other inventory to the defense industry, it came under heavy scrutiny from an environmental watchdog group. This group complained about the company's deviance from EPA-mandated policies, and the popular old generator—a cash cow for the company—was singled out as the best candidate for retooling, since it had such a high profile in the public sector. The design team worked for six months and ended up converting the generator to a one-battery system and reduced its overall size by 20 percent.

Proud of the results, the company immediately sent out press releases touting its environmentally friendly image. It even received kudos from the environmental group that had lodged the complaint because it had done such an efficient job of making sustainable modifications. However, a problem soon emerged: The generator stopped selling. Sales figures dropped so greatly and so quickly that the company decided to pull it off the shelves.

Elan, one member of the design team, decided to figure out why. He prodded his supervisor to let him do some follow-up research on the generator before the company pulled it from stores. He teamed up with his friend in the PR department, and together they designed a survey that they sent to 30 percent of the stores where sales of the generator had plummeted.

He learned that consumers were unhappy with the new generator because it ran on a single car battery that frequently gave out—leaving them without power. Even worse, the battery had a tendency to rupture inside the generator, often scorching it on the inside and leaving a dripping acidic mess on the outside.

Even though the old generator seemed less efficient and less eco-friendly because it required two batteries, it actually was much safer and more reliable.

The old generator had had no reported cases of leaking batteries and very few customer returns. In addition, Elan also learned that the smaller generator often did not fit properly into the gaskets of older RVs and trailers; it had a tendency to work its way out of the clamps and stop working.

Faced with such a poor product, many customers ended up buying a generator from the company's direct competitor—who, ironically, had produced a much less efficient version of the original generator. In other words, the company's environmentally sound retooling was sending most of its customer base to its competitor's less eco-friendly generator. When Elan shared his findings with the company, his group immediately modified the design accordingly and returned the generator to the market six months later to great acclaim—from both hunters and environmentalists.

The process of evaluating and adjusting doesn't have to be as dramatic as the above example to achieve an important effect. It can be as simple as stopping to ask your colleagues or supervisor to help you evaluate the project you've just finished. No matter how it is conducted, evaluation is really just making sure that what you're doing is helping your organization move forward—that it's real work.

A Roadmap for Action

- Make a list of what you would have to change to feel more connected to your work.

- Make a list of the people you know who do real work and make a difference in their organizations.

- Remember the consequences of not doing real work.

- Ask yourself if your personal work is aligned with the company's strategy.

- If your answer to the above question is no, think about how you can align your work with the company's strategy.

PATH 4
Understand the People Who Do the Work

Hard work spotlights the character of people: some
turn up their sleeves, some turn up their noses, and
some don't turn up at all.

—*Sam Ewing*

PATH 4 HELPS you discover your world of fake work, helps you escape from that world, and helps you do real work by discovering how the personalities of and the relationships you have with the people in your company affect the amount of fake work you and they do. In this path we explore the following questions:

- Does your personality cause *you* to do fake work?
- Does your personality cause *others* to do fake work?
- If a coworker were to team up with you, would that person be pulled into fake work?
- Are other people causing you to do fake work?

This path will discuss the character traits that cause people to do real and fake work and will help you become conscious of the influence of your personality on the work you do. Most people want to do real work, but their personalities often sidetrack them into doing fake work, causing fake work, or creating fake work.

In this chapter you'll find a list of the most common traits that promote fake work. Review them and ask yourself if you see any of these traits among your colleagues. Better yet, which of these personality traits do you see in yourself? Path 3 discussed focusing your energy on real work by taking initiative; now you'll learn to identify the personality traits of people who can help or hinder your work. The four steps covered in detail in this Path offer a framework for handling personalities at work:

Step 1: Identify your personality traits and those of your co-workers.

Step 2: Discover who you are and who you want to be at work.

Step 3: Seek and value balance, and promote behaviors that matter to others.

Step 4: Invest in people. Make changes. Follow up. Measure success.

Path 4 is important because we are all different, at least in part because of the variety of personal experiences we have had in our lives. These experiences help us develop special personality traits that guide our behavior toward others—including toward others in the workplace.

For example, if you have developed a loving and kind set of personality traits, those traits could lead you to mentor and nurture others, but they also could allow others to take advantage of you. Either way, they could lead you and your team to do fake work.

If you have a caring, nurturing personality, you may be so kind that people will do everything you ask, and what you ask could be real work. Or you may be so kind that you don't push people to do important real work, and instead allow your team members to do whatever they want—which could be fake work. Our research shows that an employee's personality, and personality traits specifically, are drivers of both real and fake work.

This is evident in the following story, in which Leslie shares her frustration as a member of a large team working on process implementation for a Fortune 500 company. She expresses concern about her project manager, Marcus, whose personality trait for group thinking and teamwork causes costly and time-consuming fake work.

TOO MANY MEETINGS,
TOO LITTLE WORK

Marcus is the ultimate group-thinker. Every time Marcus has an issue he calls a meeting. Part of me likes the idea of collaboration and keeping everyone in the loop. But this is a team of fifteen people on our side and seven on our client's side. Some meetings are attended only by our team. Some are attended by all twenty-two of us—sometimes more.

Meetings are called for everything: status check-ups, project updates, problems (of any kind), and reviews of every deliverable. In almost every case, Marcus has the best intentions behind each get-together, but the meetings are killing us. We are behind on deliverables, we are working long hours and weekends, and very few of our meetings have any purpose that justifies the hours we invest in them. In almost all cases, a few people could have talked, made decisions, and distributed information or action items to other team members—quickly.

Perhaps Marcus isn't doing the math, but the costs of these meetings are enormous. We bill the client for the meeting, and we bill the client for the hours we then have to put into the real work!

If I were making the rules instead of Marcus, we would live by the maxim "A meeting has to be really, really good to beat no meeting at all." If I've learned one thing working for Marcus, it's that if you are going to have more than two people in a meeting, it had better be important and be driven with a clear purpose. And all-inclusive meetings would have to be of extreme importance.

Good people like Leslie are drawn into fake work by other people's needs and personalities, even when they know they're being forced to waste their time. To eliminate such situations, you must learn to manage your own personality as well as others'.

What to Know About Path 4

You Can't Do it Alone

Obviously, few people work in an environment free of other people. Even a Web developer who works at home alone will have his island invaded by people periodically. And most of us work on an island that resembles Manhattan, with lots of people going in lots of directions—and all in a hurry. Dealing with people who have mad schedules in an environment of constant demands and constant change has not made things easier. And we all react differently to our circumstances based on our basic personality traits. All the knowledge and focus in the world won't ensure that you do real work if you don't pay attention to the social environment around you and how you act and interact in it.

We all have behaviors and traits that hold us back in some way or cause problems for others. And to reduce the world of fake work, we need to deal with them. You can make significant progress against the world of fake work by understanding the personality traits that positively and negatively affect your work environment. But to do so, you must know who you are and how your personality traits influence others and the work you do.

Discover How Personality Traits Could Drive Fake Work

Examining your own personality requires self-reflection, of course—but in the context of the people you work with, you work for, or who work for you. It is about how you and our fellow workers interact in your workplace—in the plant, lab, workroom, cubicle, or office. We must understand ourselves, others, and how we work together to understand how we, as individuals, as teams, or as large groups affect the value and results of our work.

An extensive list of common personality traits appears later in this section. You will no doubt recognize many of the traits—which we have paired off as opposites—in your own colleagues, and perhaps in yourself as well. But before reviewing the table, consider this story from Rebecca, a manager of a Fortune 500 company, that illustrates how important it is to be able to identify and work with the various personalities found in the workplace.

CONTROLLING POLICIES, LOSING PEOPLE

My company had a policy not to make a counteroffer to an employee who had found another job. This sort of policy may have its value, especially in businesses that basically swap employees regularly, but it ignores the endless amount of work It takes to recruit, train, and orient the employee in the first place. It also ignores the costs of losing a key player on a project or the effect of the loss on the customer.

At this company the policy seems to be championed exclusively by Chase—who is a tyrannical stickler regarding compliance. She doesn't ever rethink or reexamine the rules because, in her view, the rules are always right. And Chase makes certain that the employees who receive better offers are gone. This situation won't change until the company realizes that most of its key people have left to work for our competitors who outbid the company and recruited the company's talent away.

To me, fake work is all the work that goes into replacing employees you should and could have kept, minus the amount paid to keep them. And since the cost of replacing most employees is 40 to 60 percent of their salary, the cost of fake work is exorbitant. Rules can be dangerous. Employees can be dangerous, too—Chase's unwillingness to reexamine policies is driving this fake work.

Personality Traits That Influence Work

The chart below lists a variety of common personality traits—both negative and positive—encountered in the workplace. When examining the chart, keep the following questions in mind:

- What are your personality traits?
- What are your coworkers' personality traits?
- Do you or your coworkers' personality traits create fake work, or do they help prevent it?
- Do you and/or your team need to try to modify your personality traits to develop a more effective workplace?

Review this list of common personality traits and note the characteristics that seem to cause work problems for you and your team.

PROBLEM PERSONALITY TRAITS AND THEIR COUNTERS

Problem Personality Trait	How It Promotes Fake Work	Ideal Counter Personality Traits	How It Promotes Real Work
Aggressive	Overasserts own power and role. Creates hurt feelings and angry responses that put people on the defensive.	Peacemaker, Supportive	Pulls people back together, makes them feel valued, and keeps their energies aimed at targets.
Angry	Overreacts emotionally and hurts and alienates others. Produces negative side effects: side conversations and meetings, and bad feelings that pull people off track.	Empathetic, Calm	Helps address conflicts and keeps themselves and others focused on issues rather than emotion.
Apathetic	Disconnected and indifferent. Lacks conviction, commitment, and care about results.	Caring, Concerned, Passionate	Wants to see good things happen. Infuses energy into the workplace.

Problem Personality Trait	How It Promotes Fake Work	Ideal Counter Personality Traits	How It Promotes Real Work
Arrogant	Haughty, big-headed and won't listen. "Knows" they are always right—with or without input or data. Stubborn, cuts off input, distracts, and breaks down focus on work.	Humility, Modesty	Creates trust, passion, and motivation because humility is one of the most surprising traits of leaders and great people.
Authoritarian	Controlling, dictatorial, rigid, and severe with people. Suppresses openness and concern.	Open, Gentle, Humorous	Promotes an environment of trust and sharing that keeps people involved and contributing. Keeps work fun and builds relationships.
Bureaucratic	Paper-pushing, controlling, robotic. Puts processes, paperwork, and routine tasks above results and people.	Results-oriented, Customer-focused	Understands and focuses on the true targets of real work.

Problem Personality Trait	How It Promotes Fake Work	Ideal Counter Personality Traits	How It Promotes Real Work
Chaotic	Lacks control, clarity. Chaos can look like creativity, but actually it suppresses creativity by thwarting planning and productivity.	Organized, Disciplined	Promotes clarity, control, routines, and stability without being controlling and setting up barriers to work.
Clownish	Disrupts, interrupts, and causes endless distractions. Has an uncanny knack for moving discussions, tasks, and projects off track.	Purposeful, Focused	Prioritizes, focuses, and manages time, work, and projects with clear intent.
Confrontational	Thrives on provocation and disagreement. Negatively affects others' willingness to share, talk, and give differing opinions.	Compromiser	Invites contributions and ideas to find solutions and new approaches.

Problem Personality Trait	How It Promotes Fake Work	Ideal Counter Personality Traits	How It Promotes Real Work
Cowardly	Weak, fearful, and unwilling to confront critical issues. Avoids challenges, accepts fake work and the promoters of fake work.	Courageous	Promotes truth, focus, and strength without backing down.
Cynical	Speaks in a disparaging and negative voice that creates stagnation, poisons attitudes, negates work.	Hopeful, Optimistic	Helps people move forward, and combats setbacks and discouragement.
Debater	Constantly acts contrary and challenges every idea, which thwarts productive dialogue. Elongates meetings, creates pointless e-mail strings, and causes confusion.	Good Negotiator, Listener	Negotiates differences and finds solutions by listening intently in order to understand others.

Problem Personality Trait	How It Promotes Fake Work	Ideal Counter Personality Traits	How It Promotes Real Work
Deceptive	Avoids truth and sincerity by covering up facts and ideas, and misrepresenting statistics, products, or services. Promotes rework and doubt. Harms relationships and results through lost trust, lost business, and waste.	Authentic	Avoids masking true feelings and ideas, and builds relationships and trust by maintaining values, honesty, and truth.
Dependent	Needs constant oversight and support. Requires everyone to be present for every discussion and every decision. Neediness and lack of self-management require time from others that distracts from projects and individual work.	Independent, Interdependent	Works on problems, makes decisions within their control to ensure customers are served and projects move forward.

Problem Personality Trait	How It Promotes Fake Work	Ideal Counter Personality Traits	How It Promotes Real Work
Egocentric	Protects, promotes, and defends self above all others in all situations, which creates defensiveness and insecurity. Others will cower to avoid judgment or sabotage to seek justice.	Engaging	Connects and shows interest in work that promotes care, excitement, and the energy to work through tough times.
Enforcer and Policy Hound	Demands control, compliance, and oversight without mercy or care. Dislikes ambiguity and won't adapt to situations, which pulls managers and workers off task to comply with and arbitrate reality and rules.	Advocate	Acts as an agent for effectiveness and value. Helps find and resolve issues of concern.

Problem Personality Trait	How It Promotes Fake Work	Ideal Counter-Personality Traits	How It Promotes Real Work
Gossip Monger	Encourages careless chitchat and creates rumor, scandal, and disrespect, which drives a wedge into relationships and teams.	Respectful	Shows respect for those who are absent, talks positively, and creates camaraderie.
Group Thinker	Requires lots of discussion before making a decision. Overly cautious, avoids risk, and avoids accountability.	Action-oriented	Passionate about getting to work, meeting deadlines, maintaining focus, and getting results.
Hyperanalytical	Overanalyzes everything. Enjoys, to a fault, collecting data and doing endless research. Disregards deadlines and schedules and will delay results waiting for more information.	Balanced	Balances work, home, tasks, and emotions, which creates hope and passion. Balances behaviors, promoting creativity and adaptability.

Problem Personality Trait	How It Promotes Fake Work	Ideal Counter Personality Traits	How It Promotes Real Work
Isolationist	Works alone and avoids, even hates, teamwork. Sometimes creates secretive partners. Distracts teams and creates suspicion.	Collaborative, Teammate	Promotes collaboration, varying points of view, and creative inputs; helps others get involved and feel valued.
Lecturer	Talks at people endlessly. Avoids open-minded thought and dialogue and delivers long-winded speeches to make even simple points. Unwittingly promotes apathy and suppresses ideas.	Good Communicator	Seeks input from everyone; balances talking with listening; likes to be persuaded as well as to persuade.

Problem Personality Trait	How It Promotes Fake Work	Ideal Counter Personality Traits	How It Promotes Real Work
Malcontent, Dissatisfied, Nitpicking	Complains that nothing is good enough. Revises and wordsmiths documents forever, and usurps others' efforts. Shows no appreciation for hard work. Promotes dependency, insecurity, and anxiety.	Enthusiastic, Encouraging	Shows support, interest, and appreciation that motivates others and promotes the desire to accomplish tasks efficiently and effectively.
Manipulative	Alters facts and uses emotional warfare to get results from others. People will feel tricked and abused and will develop adaptive behaviors to avoid work and honesty.	Entrusting	Encourages people to make decisions and take responsibility, which helps others learn self-management and self-reliance.

Problem Personality Trait	How It Promotes Fake Work	Ideal Counter Personality Traits	How It Promotes Real Work
Micromanager	Seeks to control, oversee, and manage every detail. Even when delegating, makes others feel powerless by changing, adjusting, or meddling in every task. Provides a message that others are failing, so they do fail.	Empowering	Feels motivated to accomplish tasks, complete work, and carry out results. Feels valued and wants to bring value.
Multitasker	Works on several tasks concurrently with no focus on any of them. Nothing gets enough attention, which creates mediocre results for everything.	Focused, Prioritizes Well	Manages many tasks while giving each one the appropriate amount of time and attention.
Obsessive Organizer	Needs *everything* to be in place, on schedule, in order. Unrealistic expectations frustrate others. Won't change or adapt, which holds teams back.	Flexible, Resilient	Moves projects and tasks forward by finding new ways to approach them. Willing to start over, change, and innovate, which others find freeing, creative, and highly productive.

Problem Personality Trait	How It Promotes Fake Work	Ideal Counter Personality Traits	How It Promotes Real Work
Passive-aggressive	Feigns concern for others, but acts with hostility and anger. Compliant appearance is a ruse, so others lose trust. Blames others, ignores responsibility, and disregards work and decisions. Acts enthused, yet sabotages projects with a latent anger that is never expressed verbally.	Direct, Assertive	Behaves honestly, straightforwardly, and openly; gains enormous benefits because people welcome truth and fairness. Maintains open agendas and just and fair discussions, which helps people feel secure, respected, and appreciated.
Perfectionist	Works to get things perfect regardless of the situation. Strives for the unreal in a real world. Generally disappoints self and others. Fails to complete tasks, and pulls others into endless projects with ridiculous iterations.	Pragmatic	Balances a variety of needs and understands that a perfect product that fails to beat the competitor to market is perfectly fake work. Balances different concerns with attention to results.

Problem Personality Trait	How It Promotes Fake Work	Ideal Counter Personality Traits	How It Promotes Real Work
Polemicist	Sees the world as simply good and evil, black and white. Collapses in confusion in a world that is filled with ambiguity, change, adaptation, and nuance.	Adaptable	Understands that the world is constantly changing, so learns to appreciate new ideas and challenges.
Pouts, Sulks	Pouts and disconnects when not getting own way.	Engaged	Gets excited about work, challenges, and possibilities. Keeps work interesting.
Procrastinates	Avoids work, or waits until the last minute to get work done. Ignores critical tasks in favor of minutiae or delay tactics. Ignores the interdependency of work and others' needs.	Proactive	Anticipates issues and needs; gets ahead of schedule; jumps on challenges; engages in opportunities rather than reacting to issues that arise.

Problem Personality Trait	How It Promotes Fake Work	Ideal Counter Personality Traits	How It Promotes Real Work
Promotes Mediocrity	Accepts work that falls far short of the desired result and that ignores the real needs of customers and the company.	Quality-minded, Strives for excellence	Knows that excellence does not have to equal perfection, but is far from mediocrity. Conducts a careful examination of quality and connection to results that serves customers.
Self-delusional	Optimistic but lacks self-awareness. Doesn't pay attention to reality, problems, or negative patterns. Keeps people from the truth, facts, and actions required for facing and solving problems.	Realistic	Knows that people react well to a trusting environment and will help solve problems they can see and understand.

Problem Personality Trait	How It Promotes Fake Work	Ideal Counter Personality Traits	How It Promotes Real Work
Technophobe	Avoids technology and fears technology and the changes that come with it. Uses excuses to get out of performing a task that requires technology know-how.	Techno-savvy	Understands the values of technology. Seeks the best tools available but avoids superficiality and technology changes without merit.
Trivia Monger	Fills mind with trivia, data, and useless details. Focuses on the trivial rather than the big picture or the essence of issues.	Knowledgeable	Understands the difference between knowledge and information. Translates information into knowledge to solve problems and make decisions.
Tunnel Vision	Focuses on one thing to the exclusion of all else. Compartmentalizes and narrows scope to avoid responsibility, which hurts teams and divides people.	Responsible	Takes responsibility to understand the work that must be done and aligns to it. Follows through on assignments and commitments.

Problem Personality Trait	How It Promotes Fake Work	Ideal Counter Personality Traits	How It Promotes Real Work
Uncreative, Non-innovative	Works only inside the box. Ignores new ways to do things and new ideas. Remains entrenched in old systems and old processes.	Innovative, Creative	Brings new ideas and new solutions to the workplace, which can be exhilarating and satisfying.
Unreliable	Doesn't fulfill agreements. Fails to accept tasks, meet responsibilities, and deliver as promised.	Reliable	Delivers on agreements, is effective, and meets deadlines. Serves the team and the company with integrity.
Untrustworthy	Breaks down others' belief in them through many of the traits above, which hurts confidence in work and relationships.	Trust, Integrity	Exhibits behaviors that promote confidence, belief, sharing, and community.

We are all constantly dealing with people and their personality traits, which clearly affect our work. What must you do to overcome the problems caused in your work by the characteristics you possess? How are you going to deal with your coworkers' negative traits? To overcome situations where personality traits are preventing people from doing real work, follow the four steps below to move toward real work.

Steps to Move Down Path 4

Step 1: Identify Your Own and Your Coworkers' Personality Traits

Each of us has problem personality traits, and each of us has at least a few positive personality traits as well. And while we agree that it's important to focus on our positive contributions to the workplace, it's vitally important to remember that we all have personality characteristics that lead us to do fake work. With our pluses and minuses in mind, let's play a game: Ask yourself these three questions about your personality traits and the behaviors that accompany them:

1. What personality weaknesses do you have that could cause fake work?
2. What personality *strengths* do you have that, under some circumstances, could cause fake work?
3. What personality strengths do you have that help you do real work, stay focused, and avoid the pull of fake work?

Recognize your weaknesses. Consider the traits that cause you concern. These problem traits can cause fake work, as well as distress, hurt feelings, and negative attitudes, particularly as they affect others and their ability to do their jobs. Some traits may be obvious, like being angry; others are subtler, like group thinker, which may be harder to tie to fake work. Whatever they may be, your personality traits affect your relationships and your ability to work with a team. And those that are less than positive get in the way of how you focus, align, and execute your own work, not to mention how you affect the work of others.

Take a good look in the mirror. Change can happen only when you are willing to start with yourself. Also, remember that your points of view are filtered through your biases, experiences, and perceptions of the truth, so try to see yourself as others see you when examining your own traits.

Look for strengths—yours and others. Think of the positive personality traits you possess—that bring value to you, your relationships, and your work. We hope you recognized a few of them. However, research shows that we can be far too tough on ourselves. So be generous to yourself and acknowledge your good traits.

Now consider family, friends, and coworkers and find their strengths. Think of ways you could work together that would highlight these great qualities and put them to use for the benefit of your company.

Identify strengths that could turn into weaknesses. If carried to excess, some of your strengths manifest themselves as problem traits. But be careful not to jump to conclusions during this exercise. For example, you may be very organized, but that is different from being obsessively organized. And perfectionism is certainly a strength in many ways: Many inventions, discoveries, and artistic works are the products of perfectionists, whose obsessive natures pushed them to get things as close to perfect as possible.

However, perfectionism, in most practical work situations, sets up unreal expectations and interferes with teamwork, practicality, and accomplishments. In most situations, you don't need the perfect product; you need the best product that can be created within time limits. As an aeronautical engineer once told us, "The perfect plane is the plane you are developing two stages ahead of the current project, but when we get there, it will be short of what we know it could be."

As you answer the above questions, bear the following questions in mind as well:

- Where do you fall on the spectrum of effectiveness?
- How do people perceive you?
- How easy are you to work with?
- What might you be doing that gets in the way of real work?
- And most important: Are you willing to change?

Step 2: Discover Who You Are and Who You Want to Be

What is the obstacle between who you are now and who you want to become? To help answer that question, here are three questions to consider:

- What five problem traits do you want to convert to positive traits?
- What five strengths do you want to add to your current list of strengths?
- Which of your positive traits do you want to maximize?

As you answer these questions, you will begin articulating the difference between where you are and where you want to be. Then you can make a plan for developing and growing.

Some cutthroat businesspeople might say that it doesn't matter if you are a nice person so long as your personality is aiding the right work. But the fact is, being a nice person does help get work done. Angry, authoritarian, manipulative behavior has so many negative effects on yourself, other individuals, and your team as a whole that you cannot ignore the option to be kind, considerate, empathetic, and caring.

Personality Profiles Can Help You Understand Yourself and Your Relationships with Others

To help you better understand your own personality traits, try using a commercial self-assessment tool such as the well-known Myers-Briggs Type Indicator. And assessment tools in which coworkers evaluate one another, such as 360-degree surveys, are especially useful in helping you see how others perceive you.

Tests like these aren't perfect; these tools occasionally may oversimplify your traits or pigeonhole you in a way that is not completely accurate. Therefore, you should always honestly assess your behavior to see if you are actually behaving the way the instrument depicts. It's dangerous to oversimplify any data regarding the behaviors of human beings, so understand that your goal isn't to narrow your options, but to open up your options.

Completing a self-evaluation is an eye-opening, valuable, and liberating exercise. Getting to know your personality better can help you:

1. Maximize your strengths and get the best possible results.
2. Provide you with insights about why you work well with people.
3. Learn about your weaknesses and how to mitigate their negative effects.
4. Use strategies to work better with people, encourage them to do their best work and help them eliminate their own weaknesses.
5. Discover which strengths you most desire that would help you become a more balanced and effective person.
6. Improve your ability to evaluate others and appreciate their strengths.
7. Balance your interactions with others by learning to adjust your behavior to them and for them.
8. Learn how to maximize the value of others' strengths.
9. Learn the weaknesses of others and how to counter or mitigate them.
10. Understand how differences between you and those you work with necessitate different skills for communicating.
11. Open up a dialogue with your team about how to improve the quality and value of work.
12. Create a plan for personal growth and change.

THE PATHWAYS OUT OF FAKE WORK

13. Be a coach, mentor, or friend who is able to help others make positive changes in themselves.

Having successfully analyzed yourself, you now must make choices and engage your powers to make a difference.

Step 3: Seek and Value Balance, and Propagate Behaviors That Matter to Others

We have worked on an exercise with many groups of people over several years regarding wants and needs in various aspects of their lives. At the end of each session, we ask what word most symbolizes their goal. The word that comes up most often is *balance*. The more we considered this answer, the more it made sense.

A Negative Plus a Negative Creates a Negative

In the workplace, one employee's problem personality trait can instigate another problem trait. For example, an authoritarian's demanding and demeaning behavior often brings out apathetic, cynical attitudes in others. In turn, cynical, apathetic people can cause others to become authoritarian to compensate for the gaps caused by their passivity or carelessness. And cynical, apathetic people hurt communication, teamwork, and productivity. This is how negatives reinforce negatives and create a toxic workplace.

A Positive Plus a Positive Creates a Positive

Just as negatives plus negatives lead to negative outcomes, positive traits promote other positive traits. People who are open promote trust that builds collaborative and creative work. Trust helps communication, team-building, enthusiasm, and passion.

We all have strengths and we use them to bring value. Yet we all do fake work and we all have flaws—large and small. Everyone makes mistakes—we expect that and live with that. You must also realize that your behaviors cause fake work for you and your colleagues. If you are arrogant and treat people with disdain and dis-

(122)

miss their ideas, don't be surprised if you find small groups by the water cooler discussing it, or if the victims of your haughtiness have become sullen and uncooperative. Those reactions are real and perhaps honest, but they are fake work—nobody is on task for those minutes or hours when they are dealing with all their emotions. Sure, work will always have those distractions, but can you learn to minimize them through self-analysis and balancing your positives and negatives.

Step 4: Make Changes, Follow-Up, and Measure Success

The process we describe in this step can help you avoid situations like the following:

MY WAY OR MY WAY

Laura is a senior executive at a small architectural firm. She is a pedantic, egotistical bully with a lot of power, and she jumps all over most employees for very little reason. However, she is also remarkably talented, so people try to put up with her. None of this helps the business, of course, but it does feed her ego and helps justify her carelessness. And over time, many employees have paid for her outbursts. She doesn't have any gray areas—she likes you or she doesn't. If she doesn't, life will be painful until you leave.

The business is struggling because Laura interferes with everything anyone else does. Nobody feels empowered, nobody feels secure, and nobody feels committed. Only very strong, very seasoned people have their heads above water—and they are saving the business with their unyielding desire to serve customers and with their endless hope that things will change. Some of those people are deeply vested in the company, and their whole financial sustainability is at risk because of Laura.

In situations like this, the personality characteristics of one employee can easily lead to unhappiness, fake work and potential ruin for the entire company. How does one handle situations like this? By using the following process:

- *Make changes.* First figure out how *you* can change. What is getting in your way? What's keeping you from changing? These are critical questions because many of us say we should change or need to change, but we really don't have the will or courage to do the work to make it happen. Ask yourself if you are really committed, because once you are aware of a change that you need to make to become a better employee, manager, or overall person, any failure to move forward is cowardly.

If you have a Laura in your company, and you know she is causing a great deal of trouble, relationship problems, and fake work, you need to confront this issue and begin to make changes. You should first prioritize your choices regarding Laura. If, for example, you feel replacing Laura is a necessity, you need to determine where and how to begin. Get help. Do you need to talk to Laura, her supervisor, her coworkers? Realize that changing the Laura situation may take time, but by breaking down and prioritizing your options, you are taking the first critical step. Soon you will find the Laura situation less daunting.

- *Follow up, follow through.* Be consistent. Change takes time, so give it time. Suppose you get feedback from coworkers that you are arrogant and dismissive. Set up a series of tests and tasks to improve your attitude:

1. Listen to others without interrupting.
2. Ask questions and listen to responses.
3. Be open to criticism and input.

Now work on these things daily for weeks until they become habitual. Put ample time, care, and attention into making these changes.

Finally, once you feel you've changed your behavior and overcome your weaknesses, ask for input and honest feedback. Use this model for modifying any other negative behaviors you detect in yourself.

- *Invest in people.* This can be done in a simple way, and the returns are well worth the effort. Here are a few tips for promoting growth, development, and loyalty among your coworkers:

1. *Believe in people and allow them to surprise you.* They will help you gain perspective and, when you invest in your relationships, there will be a return on your investment in terms of passion, focus, and intensity. Remember, almost all our work is dependent on others.
2. *Allow others to succeed.* Set up an environment that encourages others to do well and it will end up being an environment that serves you.
3. *Involve the people around you.* In most cases, people will be generous and willing to become partners in your personal plans for growth, especially if you make it a team plan with goals and results that can be rewarding to everyone. The team will give you feedback, they will participate where they can be helpful, and they will share information and ideas with you.
4. *Hold each other accountable.* Make agreements and then ensure that you and your coworkers stick with them. Check deadlines, check quality, and check results constantly, both to help others succeed and to ensure that they are helping the team perform effectively.

- *Measure your success.* It is not easy to measure the success of your efforts to change aspects of your personality. So set up specific expectations and measures of success. Say: "I will have been successful at this endeavor if . . ." and then consider three or four things that would show success. For example, let's imagine you feel you keep yourself too isolated from your coworkers, and you realize you cover up some of your insecurities with people by lecturing them and peppering your discussions with trivia that seems to make others uncomfortable. It seems to diminish your effectiveness with people and keeps you from acting on certain issues. You want to collaborate more and be more action-oriented. Your goals and measures might be:

Goals	Measures of Success
Collaborate with colleagues.	• Created agendas for brainstorming meetings. • Brought colleagues into brainstorming sessions and everyone participated. • Didn't interrupt or distract the work. • Was validated by the participants.
Be action-oriented. Follow through.	• Ended every session with an action plan. • Ensured that the plan was written and distributed to everyone. • Followed up with each participant. • Completed work effectively and on time.
Get involved with others to accomplish work. Improve communication skills.	• Determined key tasks that must be accomplished. • Brought teammates in to address key issues and worked together to accomplish the tasks. • Communicated regularly and got feedback. • Closed meetings with clearly communicated plans. • Asked for input and received it. • Listened at least 70 percent of the time, which was validated by others.

A plan like that is not difficult to follow. It would help you better accomplish tasks, bring others into the process, and focus and prioritize work. It could even be more specific and detailed. Get serious about becoming the person you are capable of becoming. Don't minimize your ability to change, to minimize weaknesses, and to maximize strengths.

By now you should be aware of the role that personality traits play in driving both fake and real work. You've learned to review your own personality traits as well as those of your work team and make certain that they all drive real work. If your colleagues possess personality traits that are driving fake work, you know four steps for fixing the problem. You're attuned to how you behave and why, and you've gained some valuable insights on how to deal with other personalities in the workplace. So the next step is learning to communicate with your coworkers as effectively as possible, a crucial skill that is explained in the next Path.

A Roadmap for Action

- Identify the positive traits that you most want to maximize.

- Identify positive traits, as you see them, that might actually be causing others to do fake work.

- Identify your negative traits that you need to change into positive ones.

- Decide who you want to become and figure out what the gap is between where you are and who you would like to be.

- Figure out where you and others might be causing problems in your work environment.

- Determine what might be keeping you from changing.

- Establish ways to follow up and follow through to ensure that your desired change takes hold over time and makes a difference in your life and to your coworkers.

PATH 5

Communicate: Tell, Listen to, and Understand the Stories

There is no such thing as a worthless conversation
provided you know what to listen for. And questions
are the breath of life for a conversation.

—*James Nathan Miller*

PATH 5 IS about the importance of listening to the stories being told within your organization. It also highlights the benefits of bringing the sometimes hushed conversations that take place informally in hallways, restrooms, cafeterias, carpools, etc., out into the open where their value can be tapped and used to solve many fake-work situations. This path suggests that many conversations between you and your coworkers tell a larger story about how you see situations within the company.

With that in mind, you should share these stories within the organization so that others will know what is happening and can correct the issues that led to the stories. Our research in organizational communication reveals that healthy, high-performing companies are highly communicative, open companies that spend a large percentage of their time engaging in team-based, strategically aligned conversations. To help you and your company communicate more effectively, align strategically, and solve fake-work problems, follow these three steps, which we will discuss in detail in this chapter:

Step 1: Listen to what others say.
Step 2: Ensure that you understand what the stories mean.
Step 3: Use your company's stories to reduce fake work.

Path 5 provides solid reasons why communication is so important to companies. As you read each of the following statements, consider how the statement applies to you in your company and to you personally.

- Companies need to foster an open, highly communicative culture by encouraging employees to talk, to tell their stories, and to share what they know. If a company discourages discourse, a breakdown in the overall system could lead to fake work that could go on, unchecked, indefinitely.
- Companies need to create listening cultures that capture the value of the stories being told. Humans are naturally designed to talk, and companies need to develop systems to analyze and learn from their managers' and employees' stories.
- Employees typically engage in three types of conversations with one another—venting, dialogue, and strategically aligned conversations. All three types are necessary and (in most cases) healthy, but employees at highly performing companies spend a much larger portion of their time on strategically aligned conversations. Low performers get stuck "venting" or "dialoguing" with each other.
- High-performance companies help their teams align through storytelling. Teams that focus on strategic storytelling almost intuitively learn how to align themselves to real work.

The following story told by Li helps illustrate these important points:

IMPORTANT RESTROOM COMMUNICATION

I managed the customer care division of a national health care agency. We handled all the incoming calls, administered claims, and refereed complaints. Most of our claims processors worked offsite, and our core management and administrative staff consisted of twelve full-time and two part-time employees. Although our claims-processing rate was decent enough, it wasn't anything to write home about.

We weren't exactly dysfunctional, but I always sensed an undercurrent of mild dissatisfaction that I could never quite put my finger on. As I was leaving the restroom one day, I overheard a conversation between two of my coworkers. Felicia was telling Rose that she was fed up with our Mickey Mouse approval process that slowed down the processors. She said it was stupid that they had to forward their claims for preliminary approval, wait for management to return the okay, redo the claim, and then send us back the same claim, which in many cases was unmodified, for final approval. Felicia said that when she was a processor herself, she had felt that the process made her feel like her judgment wasn't valued. Now, as a supervisor, she saw that it did nothing but slow down work. She thought we really needed just one approval cycle. Rose agreed.

I remember thinking, "Gosh, I'm glad I heard that conversation." But then I stopped to ask myself, "Why haven't I heard about this before? Why did I have to learn this by accidentally overhearing a conversation in the restroom?" I had always thought I fostered an open atmosphere where employees could share their concerns, but no one had ever brought this to my attention.

When I got back to my desk and went over the approval process with a fine-tooth comb, I recognized immediately what Felicia was complaining about. She was right—it was a stupid, slow, and meaningless step. We didn't even have a good way to capture what had changed from one round to the next. It was clear this two-step approval process was hurting both productivity and morale. Ironically, our director had been telling us for years that we needed to improve our processing rate. He said it was important to the company's viability. I had listened to him but had no idea—short of cracking the whip—how to make the processors work any faster. But now I realized there was an easy way to speed up our processes and, at the same time, improve morale.

I had a wonderful discussion with Felicia reviewing this story with her and then I implemented Felicia's "restroom" ideas. Things improved dramatically in a matter of days. Our processing rate increased greatly, and we were singled out at the end of the year as the most improved division. Everyone was happy—no one more than I was. I started to wonder what other valuable suggestions might be hiding out there unknown and unheeded.

After we'd implemented Felicia's suggestions and people saw what a great success they were, individual processors and teams began to approach me with other ideas for improvement. It got to the point where we instituted a twice-monthly "conversation" in which all the groups in the division would get together to talk about how things were going and, more important, how things could be changed to improve our processing rate and how we could interact with customers more effectively.

Some people tried to use the first meeting to gripe about some personnel issues, and they had some legitimate concerns. But the rest of the teams steered them back to discussing ways to do our work better. Once people realized that this was more than just a gripe session, they really started contributing. Every team had something to offer and, as a result, everyone felt a shared responsibility for our overall success. Those talks became a critical part of our division, and because of them, our division became a star performer in the company.

Li's story shows why it's important to tell others what you see happening in your company and encourage others to do so as well. Pass on information that you think could eliminate fake work to your leaders in all regular meetings, not just to your friends in the restroom. The more good ideas you and your colleagues share, the less fake work you will do.

What to Know About Path 5

To Maintain Company Health, Communication Must Flow Freely

If you go to any company and ask, "What's your biggest problem today?" you will probably hear "communication." Lots of companies know they have huge problems communicating—people don't talk to each other, people gossip behind each other's backs, projects backfire because certain people aren't kept in the loop, and people get flooded with information but don't know what to do with it. The result: Lots of people end up doing lots of fake work.

When people stop talking to each other, teams or divisions can get factionalized and real, strategic work stops happening because, in isolation, they quickly lose track of company strategies and priorities. When communication breaks down, everyone usually knows there's a problem, and they then spend lots of time talking about the issues—in the hallway! "Can you believe how incompetent he is?" "I can't believe we're going to be doing this initiative again. Don't they know how stupid it is?" "What is our executive team doing redesigning our strategy for the third time?"

Many corporate executives view "communication" as an omnipresent illness because the hallways of their offices are filled with nonproductive banter. Frequently they will try to "cure" this problem with one of these faulty tactics:

- Discouraging venting or other communication by fostering a "shut up and get back to work" mindset.
- Hiring outside consultants to analyze their corporate culture.
- Instituting performance reviews to help individual employees move past their perceived behavioral problems.
- Communicating their strategic decisions to everyone through internal newsletters or intranet Web pages (that are all too often ignored).
- Holding sporadic roundtable discussions to air grievances.

Because companies tend to view hallway conversations as problems or irritants that need to be fixed, they often end up focusing on eliminating the "wrong" kind of conversation and promoting the "right" kind of open communication. But in plenty of instances, these "corrective" measures don't really do anything to foster better communication or build an open, honest environment where people know what's happening and how their work aligns with key company priorities. In fact, the measures often end up having the opposite effect: They stifle the actual conversations about work that need to happen!

Companies are complex organisms that require the free flow of information to every nook and cranny of the organization. When companies become too heavily invested in monitoring, formulating, eliminating, or prescribing certain kinds of communication, they place unnatural burdens on natural human methods of exchanging information. The best thing companies can do is build a vibrant and highly communicative environment that actually is open, not just socially engineered to *feel open*. This may sound like a difficult thing to accomplish, but in fact, the solutions are sometimes quite simple, as you'll see in Josh's story.

CELL PHONES SAVED THE DAY

My company, which created and supported high-tech systems, had a communication problem that escalated to the point where management could no longer ignore it. So a group of outside consultants was brought in to analyze the problem. After months of "listening" to the employees, taking surveys, and conducting focus groups, the consultants delivered a scathing report that detailed how the organization was split into silos of information that remained locked away behind divisional doors. The consultants then recommended that the silos be eliminated by capturing and standardizing all of our technical procedures in a hard-copy manual.

That process took another six months, and finally the consultants came forward with a giant manual that no one in the company felt any ownership of. It soon ended up tossed in the back seats of service vehicles and gathering dust in cubicles.

Despite being given what was derisively dubbed "The Bible," technicians were still making two or three trips to a client to fix problems, and the time-to-completion rate for projects wasn't getting any better. At a follow-up meeting three months after the Bible's launch, our executive team concluded that things had actually gone from bad to worse.

During the follow-up discussion, one divisional VP suggested that, as a stopgap measure, we buy all the technicians cell phones so that they could at least help each other out with questions while they were out on repair calls. This provisional, ad hoc fix actually became the solution. Why? Because the repair staff did what comes naturally to all of us—they began talking to each other and sharing information in real time. The cell phones created an informal, highly communicative environment where information, ideas, and experiences could be shared on the spot.

Morale improved, and our time-to-completion rate on service calls improved by 40 percent. Not because of a very expensive manual, but because people started talking.

Although manuals are often necessary within organizations, in this case the manual became a congealed form of fake work because it wasn't useful. The cell phones got people to talk—and the talk reduced fake work.

Listen to the Stories Where You Work

High-performance companies understand the value of listening and find ways to use what they learn as they listen. They're able to retain value from company stories because they understand a deep truth about the workplace: that people at work tend to operate as storytellers, and the stories they share capture the value of work in a kind of company currency that everyone in the company can use, save, waste, or spend.

Companies are filled with people who tell tales about how a certain project succeeded against all odds, about how the company treats its employees as if they were family, about how a certain group of people made huge sacrifices and dedicated themselves tirelessly to make sure a new product line rolled out on time, or how the founders started out with nothing but the shirts on their backs and made it big through solid, hard work.

They're also filled with people who tell tales about how nothing ever seems to go right for a particular division, about how the CEO has an ax to grind and will never be satisfied, about how the company is sucking the life out of its employees, or about how the company doesn't prepare people to perform their jobs properly.

The stories can be as disparate and varied as anything you'd imagine, and they are either the lifeblood or the clogged arteries of the company. They encapsulate a company's history, its point of view, its personality, its predictable set of behaviors, and its culture. Stories can tell you what a company thinks about itself, where it sees its own value and the value of its competitors, how it thinks it contributes to the market, and even why the company got started in the first place. They can tell you what has happened in the past, what the company thinks about its history, and what will probably happen in the future. Stories aren't scientific—they're autobiographical, and they are inestimably valuable because they deliver a complex and compelling context of personal opinions, beliefs, and gut feelings. In effect, stories are a great indicator, and in some ways the most reliable indicator, of the company as a whole and of specific issues such as fake work.

Companies that listen to what their stories have to say, and then act upon what they learn, help keep work based in reality. The most important thing that a company can do is listen to the stories as they are told and then learn what they need to do to help drive the work to more successful ends.

You can discover and eliminate fake work as you tap into the stories of your workplace and become aware of what is happening. And to do that, you must listen to the people you work with, and you must understand the meaning of the stories they tell you.

The following three key steps will guide you to becoming an effective listener, communicator, and user of company stories.

Steps to Move Down Path 5

Step 1: Listen to What Others Say

To understand the meaning of stories, you first must listen to them. The critical element in listening is to focus on the other person instead of yourself (particularly what you want to say next) to learn what the person thinks, feels, and means. While listening, avoid speaking except to encourage the other person to continue.

Good listening places the responsibility of continuing a conversation, dialogue, or interview on the other person. If you ask, "What do you think about the work you are doing?" and then look intently and inquiringly at the person you're addressing, the responsibility for continuing the dialogue is placed firmly on the person. The commitment to communication is equally strong when you simply say "uh-huh" or "hmmm" when the other person makes a comment. And the effect is essentially the same when you echo the idea that the other person has just stated. When you respond in these ways, you create an expectation that can be fulfilled only when the other person talks and when you listen.

The following dialogue illustrates this approach:

Susan: Judy, how do you feel about the work we do in this department?

Judy: Working in this department is extremely frustrating.

Susan: Hmmm.

Judy: What I mean is that I'm fed up with doing work that no one uses or cares about and that doesn't help the company.

Susan: Uh-huh.

Judy: You know what I mean—they quit using our report six months ago.

Susan: They quit using the report six months ago?

Judy: That's right! The company quit using the report, but they haven't even told us to stop working on it.

Susan: What do you think could be done to resolve this situation?

This approach to listening is grounded in the theory of positive reinforcement. People like to talk to others who support them or at least do not dismiss or reject them. Reinforcement theory suggests that a person's behavior is influenced by its consequences. Thus, if you react or respond in a supportive manner to something the other person said, he will feel that his comments have been reinforced, and will continue to talk. Each of these listening responses provides positive reinforcement by indicating that you have an interest in what the other person is saying, and that you care enough to listen. And they cause *you* to hear the stories.

But despite their proven effectiveness, these listening techniques will work only if the questioner sincerely wants to hear what the speaker has to say. If the listener is not genuinely interested, the speaker usually senses what is happening and then refuses to cooperate, focusing instead on the insincere technique rather than on communication. Keep in mind that the combination of facial expressions, tone of voice, and body language plays a vital role in listening.

Step 2: Ensure That You Understand What the Stories Mean

Having heard the stories, you need to make sure you understand them. To do that, it helps to restate in your own words what the other person's words mean to you. Then, the other person can determine whether the message getting through to you is the one he or she intended.

When you express your understanding, you indicate to the other person how you have interpreted his or her statements and feelings. That in turn prompts the person to clarify, expand on, or further explore those ideas and feelings. Often the person then moves on to express a new idea or feeling.

Step 3: Use Your Company's Stories to Make Change

When you can hear and understand the stories shared within your company, you have the information necessary to begin reducing fake work and increasing real work. As we mentioned earlier in the chapter, employees tend to engage in three types of conversations with one another: venting, dialogue, and strategically aligned conversation. Examining which type of conversation you're hearing and what, exactly, your colleagues are saying and feeling will reveal what sort of changes need to be made.

Venting

Venting consists primarily of griping about problems that are largely interpersonal in nature. Its primary purpose is the release of anxiety, anger, insecurity, pent-up energy, ill will, or animosity, all with the hope of returning safely to the normal state of any given working situation. Healthy venting allows employees to feel that their needs are being recognized and that they are free and open to say what bugs them. Unhealthy venting can range anywhere from constant griping about the same problem to people crying and running out of the office.

These statements are typical examples of venting:

- "I think I'm getting overlooked and I know I could really contribute to this project. They just need to put me on the team."
- "I'm fed up with Bill's incompetence. I don't know what he's thinking."
- "Jane really screwed up this report. Can't she get fired already?"
- "Don't talk to me about growth. This company is totally short-sighted and will cut us all off at the knees. No wonder people are suspicious of every change."
- "This is the dumbest idea I've ever heard. He's on crack if he thinks this will work."

It's important to remember that even though venting sometimes seems unhealthy, it can be a valuable source of strategic information if you can learn to listen to what's really being said underneath all the emotion.

Dialogue

Just as venting often contains strategic information, dialogue does as well, though it often needs to be translated more specifically back into the explicit language of strategy. Dialogue consists primarily of neutral, objective discourse that often surrounds project planning, brainstorming, or executing tasks. It's the most common kind of language we use in a given day, and it's basically functional, interactive storytelling. Dialogue is communication that can help work move forward in a productive, effective way. But it can also devolve into simple cover-your-behind-speak and full-fledged justifications and rationalizations.

Dialogue often consists of statements like these:

- "Cathy will finish off the pre-press work on Tuesday, and we should have the final proof ready for Larry by Friday."
- "I had planned to get you those figures by Friday, but I had to spend more time on the estimates because of the labor shortage."
- "My sense of this project is that it lacks information; until you've had a chance to revisit your thoughts about these numbers, I'll wait before I calculate the final results."
- "I was following Devon's mandate that we not do more work on the project until the contract was signed. If Devon hadn't put up such a fuss, we would have had more time to work on the project."
- "This project may have been compromised from the get-go because we didn't really have buy-in from the stakeholders. But, that's not my fault. I did everything I could to make this project a success."

When translated by a perceptive, sensitive team or an excellent manager, dialogue can be deciphered to reveal what the employee or team is trying to say about strategy.

Strategically Aligned Conversation

Strategically aligned conversation consists of focused, relevant, and work-related stories, almost always taking place in a team-based setting, which helps the participants understand a situation in the context of company strategy. It transforms the concerns of both venting and dialogue into insight that leverages value by linking concerns, issues, and ideas to strategy. Strategically aligned conversation resembles the following statements:

- "Our approval process is dramatically lengthening our time-to-completion rate because it's adding in an unnecessary step. If we want to improve our rate and help the company, we need to eliminate this pointless rubber-stamping."
- "If we really do need to grow our sales by 15 percent over the next two quarters, we need to make sure that Manufacturing can support the increased demands our project would entail."
- "We're getting hindered by the lack of compatibility between Karl's designs and Frieda's modifications. If we're going to make this process work, we've got to sit back down and make sure the engine is really doing what it needs to do."

Every Conversation Says Something About Strategy

Every piece of conversation, every article of information, and every story shared says something about strategy. But that doesn't mean it's always easy to grasp what's strategic about a given story; that requires subtlety, sensitivity, and a deep commitment. But it's worth the effort. Even when it sounds as if your coworkers are whining, there is value in what they are saying. The griping going on in Accounting isn't because they're all bad eggs—maybe it's because they're being forced to do tons of fake work on budgets they know will never be accepted by the board. The discussions emanating from the marketing department that never succeed in creating a compelling set of campaign materials aren't because the marketing team comprises a bunch of lackluster individuals—maybe they've been overwhelmed by redesigning the corporate recruitment brochure for the third time in two years to reflect major changes in strategic imperatives. Or maybe the board of directors isn't ineffective but, rather, trying too hard to please an indecisive and fickle CEO. Whatever is behind the stories, it's critical that you translate them into solutions for reducing fake work and increasing real work.

Allow natural patterns of communication to happen, but also constantly strive to link the information content of the communication back to the work you are doing.

A Roadmap for Action

- Determine whether your company is closed and secretive or whether it is open and highly communicative.

- Open your ears at work. What kinds of stories do you hear in your hallways?

- Are the stories told within your organization mostly venting, dialogue, or strategy?

- What stories might your work team tell about the work it does?

- Reflect on the stories you hear at work and analyze what the stories are teaching you about both fake and real work.

PATH 6
Teams Drive Real Work

Teamwork is the ability to work together toward
a common vision. The ability to direct individual
accomplishments toward organizational objectives.
It is the fuel that allows common people to attain
uncommon results.

—*Andrew Carnegie*

PATH 6 IS about how to see yourself in the context of the team you're a part of and of your company as a whole. This may come as a shock, but quite often individual team members working side by side do not really know what the other team members do. But when team members realize what their partners really do, productivity skyrockets. They notice the overlaps and see that critical work is not being done. Fake work in teams is then reduced—almost "magically"—as team members discover how they each relate to one another and that they are not individuals doing "their work" but a team working together toward important strategic goals.

This path will provide you with three steps to help reduce fake work that is created and driven by work teams:

Step 1: Make certain your team understands company strategy.
Step 2: Discover the connectedness between team members.
Step 3: As a team, help each team member align his or her work with company strategy.

Path 6 is important and exciting because it shows how to start eliminating fake work on a macro level. It teaches you how to streamline and reduce fake work, and will strengthen your team in the process. You'll see what your team's strengths and weaknesses are, and learn to fix what you're doing wrong—such as failing to meet regularly to discuss how work tasks align with strategic goals. The following story illustrates what can happen when a team lacks regular update meetings:

TEAMWORK REDUCES FAKE WORK

We recently did some consulting work in Europe with a large, multinational fast-food company. During this time, its operation in one European country was asked to predict how many new drive-through restaurants the group could open in the country during the coming year.

Lars, the director for the company in question, quickly met individually with most of his management team members in the country and then told corporate headquarters that the company would open twenty drive-through restaurants over the next twelve months. We met with this team about two weeks after Lars made this commitment, but we were unaware that it had been made. We completed an exercise with the team in which the team members discussed their roles with each other and described their individual work tasks. It was interesting to learn how little they knew about each other's roles and the specific work assignments they completed. They discovered that three or four people were doing the same work tasks—a huge waste of time—and that several important assignments were simply not being done by anyone.

But the most upsetting news came when the team member specializing in property acquisition learned for the first time that Lars had committed to opening twenty new drive-through restaurants. He explained to the group that the government would allow our company to acquire only ten pieces of property per year for fast-food restaurants. This information shocked the team, as they were all moving forward with plans to open the twenty new restaurants: The person in charge of construction had already purchased many of the materials for twenty new buildings. The HR person was in the midst of the process of hiring and training managers for twenty locations. The marketing people were getting marketing packets ready for all twenty restaurants as well as for a large national campaign announcing the openings. Indeed, everyone was excitedly working with the number twenty in their minds. At that moment, they all realized they were doing a great deal of costly and meaningless fake work.

What caused this fake work and this major misunderstanding? The lack of regular team meetings where the work was discussed! Too often individuals go on their merry way doing what they think needs to be done and exclude the rest of the team. Lars committed this fatal error. He did not bring the team together and use the team effectively to begin with, and this caused misunderstandings to occur and costly fake work to be done.

In the end, the corporate office was furious about the missed commitment. Lars was mad at his team and particularly the land acquisition member because he should have made all team members aware of the situation much sooner. In fact, Lars left the company within two weeks of our team training.

We wish we could say that this sort of situation happens infrequently. But we see issues like this all the time. It would be easy to view this circumstance as a description of an ineffective boss who did not coordinate well with his acquisition team and the rest of the team. That's true, but that's just half the story: If the team had been meeting regularly, this problem would never have occurred, because it would have heard from the land acquisition specialist early on. When teams interact, they broaden their knowledge and they save themselves and their leaders from fake work.

What to Know About Path 6

You Are an Individual, but You Belong to a Team

It is crucial to realize that each of us is a member of many teams and that each of these teams influences who we are, and we in turn influence what each team becomes. You can maintain a strong sense of self, but you must understand how this self fits into the team. The French psychoanalytic thinker Jacques Lacan has a theory that nicely explains how this principle works. Lacan theorizes that children become conscious of themselves *as selves* only when they are able to recognize themselves in a mirror—between six and eighteen months of age. Lacan calls this the "mirror stage" and suggests that once we are able to recognize ourselves in the mirror, we become conscious human beings with a vested place in the world of human affairs. He believes that our entrance into the "mirror stage" indicates that we have entered a "symbolic order" that provides us with a sense of self-definition and tells us who we are. Lacan's symbolic order has important consequences for us as individuals because it tells us what things mean, how we ought to behave, and what our world looks like.

In Lacan's theory, we don't just awaken to ourselves, we awaken to the fact that we are selves in an ongoing world. If I'm Lisa Simpson, I don't awaken to my essential Lisa-ness. Instead, I awaken to the fact that I am a girl child in a family of five. My dad is horribly incompetent and works at a nuclear power plant where he routinely causes toxic accidents. My brother, Bart, is a class clown and is constantly getting into trouble because he does stupid things like burn the Christmas tree down. My mom has a tower of blue hair and wears the same Wilma Flintstone–like dress every day. I am smarter than almost everyone around me, and I play the saxophone. I am Lisa precisely because of this exact set of personal and social circumstances that gives me the role of "Lisa" to play.

In other words, we don't just learn that we *are*, we learn that we are someone because we are a part of an interconnected world of relationships. Our symbolic order gives us the sense not just that we exist, but that we exist embedded in a wide circle of human relationships that are circumscribed by language, people, social systems, and complicated meanings. Lacan's theory about the mirror stage offers great insight about the workplace and why so many of us do so much fake work. Lacan's basic point is this: To understand yourself in a true way, you have to understand how you fit into and are created by the social order around you.

In our work environment the social order can be the entire organization, but more specifically it consists of the people we interact with daily: our work team. This team usually represents those we rub shoulders with daily, have lunch with, see on coffee breaks, interact with in team meetings, and work together with on projects. And teams have a great impact on how we work and how much fake work we do.

Being Part of Your Work Team While Eliminating Fake Work

At work people tend to think only of themselves and their individual efforts, and disregard their work teams. It's easy to think, "I am the work I do, and I expend personal effort to complete it." We may acknowledge that we work in a team in concert with other people, but it's easy to slip into the mode of thinking that our work is the output of our own personal energy. "I am the CEO because I paid my dues." "I am a mid-level manager, and I am good at my job because I understand systems and processes." "I am the newest hire at the organization, and I am not certain if I am qualified for this job." We often fail to think of the work team that shapes us and helps to define us. Your perceptions about the work you do and how you do that work is what keeps you returning to work day after day, year after year. And if you feel that, personally, you're contributing to something bigger than yourself, you feel good about the work you're doing and often strive to do a better job.

Your individual perception is only one side of your work story, though. In reality, work always happens as a product of individual effort within a team of people. In other words, individuals do their respective work tasks, but the work they do has meaning only if it integrates well with everyone else's work in the company. If your work does not integrate with the work of other team members, chances are you are doing fake work, work that is not aligned with team or company strategy.

The following story illustrates the importance of teamwork and alignment with strategy.

FERRARI WINS SIX CONSTRUCTORS' CHAMPIONSHIPS

Earning approximately $40 million per year, Michael Schumacher was once the highest-paid athlete in the world and regarded as the greatest Formula One driver ever. Before his retirement in 2006, he helped Ferrari win six Constructors' Championships in a row and dominated the race circuit from the mid-1990s up to his retirement by winning an unprecedented seven Drivers' Championships.

Ferrari and Schumacher made winning look easy. They rarely made a mistake, they were able to completely change their racing tactics mid-race to accommodate unexpected developments, and they almost always won. So what separated them from the other teams that, in theory, had the same access to weather reports, bought the same tires, and subscribed to the same F1 technical specifications and regulations?

The Ferrari difference! Then and now, every member of the Ferrari team is flexibly aligned to every other member of the team, and the team as a whole is focused on a crystal-clear strategy. To watch a Ferrari pit stop is to witness an elegantly choreographed dance where the driver gets fluids, the wheels get replaced, and fuel gets added all on cue. The team does no more or less than every other team, but their pit stops are routinely two or three seconds faster. Every team member's tasks are honed and refined to shave off tenths of a second, to be absolutely precise, to be delivered in an optimally efficient way, and to be perfectly aligned with what everyone else is doing. Everyone on the Ferrari team works at optimum capacity with a purely strategic goal, and their accumulation of quarter-seconds here and half-seconds there is responsible for their consistent superiority at the checkered flag.

Lots of people mistakenly think that Ferrari wins because it has the biggest budget and the best driver, but all you have to do is listen to Schumacher singing his team's praises from the winner's podium week after week to understand that teamwork is what really makes Ferrari tick. Even when it raced in 1999 with an inferior car and a substitute driver for Schumacher, Ferrari still won the championship because its highly aligned team made up for both technological and driver deficits. They're so well aligned that they can leverage value where other teams can't even begin to see it.

The same type of success stories happen off the racetrack as well. However, many organizations build team-oriented, performance-driven cultures that try to achieve teamwork, but don't do enough to help their teams focus on strategy and eliminate fake work.

All organizations share one overriding strategic goal: blending distinct personalities and work styles so employees can work together to accomplish work tasks that lead to intended results. That doesn't mean all team members have to look, act, and think alike; it just means they have to be able to mesh together in a functional, strategic way, with the company's key goals at the forefront of their consciousness.

Are Your Work Tasks Aligned with Your Work Team?

Everyone has something to contribute to a company, but no single person can successfully contribute anything if his or her efforts aren't aligned to the team's and the company's strategic goals. It doesn't matter whether you're the CEO, a regional VP, a marketing executive, a team supervisor, or a line worker: Your work tasks have to be aligned to company strategy to make a difference. Otherwise, your own value within the workplace is diminished.

So how do you know if your work is aligned? You have to be

able to see yourself within the context of your team and your company and ascertain if the work you do is directly related to the health and strategy of the business's core concerns. And that's not always easy to do.

Sometimes bad alignment is the fault of your company because it hasn't done a good job of identifying and articulating its strategy. Other times, it might be your or your team's fault because you know the strategy but you haven't paid any attention to it. Sometimes someone more powerful than you will make you do something because somebody else is pushing for it—even though everyone knows it's not related to strategy. And occasionally, it's simply your fault because you're the CEO and you've put a strategy in place but you're making your staff work on something else.

The worst part about being misaligned is that often you have no real way of knowing that the work you're doing is misaligned and therefore meaningless to the company. In fact, you could be working hard, feeling good about the work you're doing, and really trying to be creative and innovative in your methods. You might even feel you've found a real purpose in the work you do, and you'd be offended if someone told you that you were doing fake work. But you might well be putting a lot of effort and energy into nothing. Consider the example of Jane, a newly hired training developer.

ALIGNING WORK WITH COMPANY GOALS

Jane was a technology whiz who was hired as part of a training and development team. During her initial interview with her team, she was told her job would be mission-critical to the team and was told how important it was that she help develop its online offerings, since the company wanted to begin integrating online and distance learning (courses that employees could complete alone on the computer) into the core company training offerings.

Jane took this charge seriously, and after six months she had increased the division's online offerings by more than 30 percent and had a 50 percent increase in online enrollment. She was proud that she had focused all her efforts on the things her team had emphasized.

Unfortunately, Jane's team had seriously misled her: The company's top priority was increasing its annual growth by 10 to 15 percent, while Jane ended up costing the company money because the development costs of the online training were very high. This was really not her fault. It was the team's fault. The team was misaligned with the strategic goals of the company. When higher-ups told Jane she was a drain on resources, intentionally or not, she got angry and quit. In her exit interview, she claimed that she was "just doing the job I had been hired to do." Unfortunately, through no fault of her own, it was all fake work. And what was even more unfortunate is the fact that her team should have known it.

Work teams that are not in touch with the strategy of their company are quite common. They push forward doing all kinds of work that does not meet the strategic goals of the company. The training team's failure to align their work with the company's strategy ended up costing Jane her job.

You must work to change things at both the individual and team level by focusing your work efforts on company strategy. You might not be able to completely and fully align yourself with your team and your company, but you can make a huge difference by making sure your work tasks are connected to your company's critical strategies. Jane could have questioned how her new role worked toward achieving her company's goals, but she was never made aware of what the company's strategy was.

What can you do to make certain your work tasks are aligned with your team and with your company's strategic goals? These three steps can help you work effectively with your team and fight fake work.

Steps to Move Down Path 6

Step 1: Make Certain Your Team Understands Company Strategy

A team can be defined as a small group of people engaged in a common venture, a division, a business unit, or the entire company. However large or small, teams need to focus on doing work that is aligned to critical strategies that help companies perform and succeed; otherwise, they risk being completely irrelevant.

Unfortunately, most teamwork processes are neither about teams nor about work. And intuitively, when teams sense that the work they do is meaningless, irrelevant, or destined to fail, they get mired in destructive patterns. Sure, there are some teams that fail simply due to incompatible personalities or styles, but we think a large percentage of teams are rendered ineffective by a lack of clear, strategic focus. When teams can't understand what effect their work will have or what a successful result would look like, they inevitably look for a different way to evaluate themselves and the scope of their work, which shifts the target from where it should be. They end up focusing on their internal team dynamics or their own self-perceptions about how they're working, because they sense that their work doesn't count for much of anything. You could have the best people in the world on your team, but if the team is not aligned to critical strategy, its work will still amount to nothing in the final analysis.

Review the following checklist to analyze whether your team is aligned:

- I know the strategy of my company.
- I know the strategy of my team.
- I know what tasks I do that further the strategy.
- I know how the tasks of each of my team members further the strategy.

If you can't answer each of these statements with a "yes," you are likely not aligned with the strategy of your team and your company. The next step will help you make certain not just that your team is aligned with company strategy, but also that each member is doing important work.

Step 2: Discover the Connectedness Between Team Members

Whenever we work with teams, we always have them complete an assignment in which the entire team reviews the work of each team member. First, we ask each team member to explain to the rest of the team what he or she does during an average workweek. Then, when team members are finished with their presentations, they ask each other questions.

This exercise inevitably results in discussions about why people do what they do and how their work overlaps with someone else's work on the team. As we've mentioned, most team members are not very aware of what, specifically, other team members do on a regular basis, and this lack of awareness leads to a great deal of fake work.

LET THE FIELD KNOW ABOUT THE HAIR CARE MARKETING CAMPAIGN

Leda, Bev, and Ron were members of a project team that was asked to develop a marketing campaign for their company's newest hair care product. Each member of the project team was selected because of a special ability: Leda was chosen for her innovative and creative style; Bev was picked because of her writing skills and because she was the team leader's administrative assistant; and Ron was selected because of his design skills. The five other team members possessed valuable individual strengths as well.

Because each team member represented a different department, they had all been instructed to let their people know what was happening on the campaign. The team leader, Richard, was adamant that everyone throughout the company know what was happening at all times.

Richard asked Leda to send regular e-mail updates about the campaign to everyone in the company. Bev assumed that as Richard's assistant, she should be letting everyone know what was happening with the team each week. Ron, who considers himself the best communicator in the company, took it upon himself to send a weekly e-mail to everyone with news about the campaign.

After the team had been working together for about three months, they met with a consultant who asked them each to describe their assignments and the work they did in an average week to the other team members.

When the team discovered that Leda, Bev, and Ron were each sending updates about the work of the team, they were surprised and disappointed. Because of the overly abundant e-mails flying around, few were being read and most were ignored. Obviously, two of them were doing fake work! The team members wanted to blame Richard, but it was not Richard alone who caused this; the team needed to share the responsibility. Leda, Bev, and Ron were particularly unhappy, and they began to resent having been assigned to the team.

Redundant work occurs within countless teams. On the other hand, there are many situations where important tasks are not being done by anyone. Whether you and your team are doing overlapping work or are not doing critical tasks, you are either doing fake work or failing to do real work.

So how do you ensure your team is on track? The following short process will help you get better aligned as a team and lead to more real work.

1. *Have regular meetings.* Hold regular meetings to review each team member's work assignments.
2. *Discuss work assignments.* Have each team member share what he or she does in a normal week.
3. *Questions and answers.* Allow time for the rest of the team to review and ask questions regarding the other team members' work.

4. *Review overlaps and tasks not being done.* Make certain there are no work overlaps and that all necessary tasks are being completed.

Step 3: As a Team, Help Each Member Align Work with Strategy

Knowing what each team member is actually doing is vitally important in helping your team align with strategy. Clearly, individuals do the work of a company, and it is crucial that they feel they have a part in selecting the work they do. Employees can usually determine what tasks they should do if the team leader is constantly reviewing the organization's and the team's strategy with the team members.

Ensure That Alignment Is Owned by Individuals

Alignment is an issue that must start with leadership, but the responsibility to be aligned must be owned by individuals in the team at the work level. And alignment cannot be thrust onto people—people must align themselves through the lens of the team.

For many years, people have talked about alignment and its importance to organizations. Then, as for many other problems, they put the responsibility on leaders and not on individuals and teams. This is not the way to solve the problem. Here are some conditions critical to aligning a company:

1. Leaders must sponsor alignment, but they can't make it happen.
2. Leaders are collaborators in alignment, but they can't solely drive alignment.
3. Alignment is a people issue. It's about how employees work with and value each other.
4. Alignment is based on behavior. Workers must clarify their behavior and make sure they're doing the right work.
5. Alignment requires continuous and valuable communication

regarding how each individual's work fits within the context of the team.

Ways to Guarantee That Work Is Aligned to Strategy

Teams can ensure that all members' work is aligned by:

1. Clarifying, translating, and defining company strategies.
2. Asking all workers to define their critical tasks, and separating those tasks from mundane tasks, which still have to be done.
3. Prioritizing and refining critical tasks.
4. Aligning critical tasks with other players to establish a cohesive focus and a team-based approach for completing strategic goals.
5. Building work plans to hold each other accountable.
6. Monitoring work plans and reviewing them to ensure they are real over time.
7. Holding each other accountable for sticking to work plans.

Hold a Work Team Alignment Session

A work team session is a meeting with all team members to help them align their work with the team and the company. The key to a successful work team session is to remember that participation in a work session is not a retreat from the daily realities of work. Instead, it's an opportunity to dig deeper into the realities of work and emerge with a realistic plan for how you and your team can best contribute to the company's strategic goals. Here are the five steps of the alignment process that take place in a work team session:

Step 1. Relating Your Work Tasks to Company Strategy

Objective: Understand your company's strategic goals and begin to connect your daily work tasks to those goals.

Approach: All team members, including the team leader, should share their understanding of the organization's vision, mission, and strategy. This step helps them establish a clear relationship between company strategy and their work tasks. And it helps them see the difference between what they *are* doing and what they *should* be doing to support the company's strategic goals.

Step 2. Identifying Your Critical Work Tasks

Objective: Identify the tasks that will allow you to best help your company reach its strategic goals.

Approach: With the company's strategic goals in mind, have each team member determine which tasks must be completed within a set time frame. Ask the team members to respond to the following questions: "What work must I accomplish during the next few months to keep my boss, fellow employees, customers, and other company members happy? What can I do to make sure I feel personal growth and satisfaction? What is the strategic relevance of each of these tasks?"

Step 3. Establishing Your Priorities and Aligning Tasks

Objective: Validate your work tasks and their relationship to your company's strategic goals with input from your team.

Approach: Solicit input from teammates to verify that the tasks you see as most critical are indeed the most important in terms of team priorities and company strategy.

Step 4. Developing Your Individual Work Plan

Objective: Commit to a realistic work plan that allows you to accomplish your work tasks and contribute to your company's strategic goals.

Approach: Translate your work tasks into specific actions. Create a work plan that specifies short- and long-term steps for accomplishing your most important work tasks.

Step 5. Following Up

Objective: Check up on your progress and identify any required modifications to your work plan.

Approach: The team should hold regular meetings to determine how each team member is doing with their work plan and to help them make modifications as necessary. Constantly assess the execution of your work plan. By making any necessary course corrections and recommitting to your work, you increase the likelihood that you will successfully complete your work tasks.

The challenge presented in this path is for you and your team to make the effort to align your work with that of other team members and with the company's strategic goals. If you do, you will reduce the amount of fake work that you do. Now that you know how to assess whether you and your team are aligned with your company's strategy, you are well on your way to winning the battle against fake work. In the following chapters we'll examine how leaders can tackle fake work from the top.

A Roadmap for Action

- Identify the true purpose of your company.

- Make sure you understand your company's strategic goals.

- Figure out how you provide value to the strategy.

- Determine your role as a steward within the company.

- Think about how you would describe your team. Do you and your team members know your company's strategy and how your work contributes to the execution of the strategy? Do you know what your team members do on a day-to-day basis? Do they know what you do?

PATH 7
Close the Execution Gap to Drive Real Work

Leaders spend nowhere near enough time trying to
align their organizations with the values and visions
already in place.

—*Jim Collins*

PATH 7 IS about the process that links strategy to alignment to execution. This path explores the importance of developing and communicating company strategy, aligning individuals and work teams to the strategy, and executing the strategy to attain the results the company needs to succeed.

Strategy helps define the critical focus and the shifts and adjustments a company needs to make to respond to customer and market demands. As you now know, real work is work that is linked to strategy, but strategy has no value if it can't be seen in the actual work itself.

The "execution gap" is the metaphorical space that exists between strategy and execution. Path 7 will show you how to close the gap by implementing each of the following steps:

Step 1: Make your strategic planning and implementation process real.
Step 2: Create and articulate strategies that can be turned into work.
Step 3: Communicate company strategies effectively to employees.
Step 4: Close the "execution gap"—the chasm between strategy and work.
Step 5: Do the work itself with precision, and measure it.

Path 7 integrates the three elements of real work that drive the success of a company: strategy, alignment, and execution. Failing to focus on *all* these elements is a recipe for fake work, and balancing all three is an absolute necessity.

A common and very serious mistake companies make is to think of strategy, alignment, and execution as distinct and separate processes. An even bigger mistake is to think responsibility for these processes lies solely with the company's leaders. All three of these interlinking processes require the involvement of all employees in the company. High-performance companies know that and ensure they act in alignment with the following three principles:

1. Strategies are critical to company focus and must be developed in accordance with the best ideas of the company from top to bottom.

2. Individuals and teams must have their work seamlessly aligned to the strategy.

3. Execution is the proof that strategy is understood and carried out at the point of work—where effort meets performance and results.

In the following story, Jackie describes her experience of joining a relatively young, fast-growing medical products company as the vice president of operations. Before she even came on board, she read everything she could about the company—and made some interesting discoveries.

LOTS OF WORK WENT INTO THIS CHAOS

I was excited about joining the company. It was doing well and overflowing with talent and ideas. With a couple of patented products approved by the FDA, they had taken off and built a business from the ground up. Now, ten years later, they were somewhat stable, somewhat profitable, and growing fast.

However, they were just pushing into that zone where they had to respond to the growth and the complexity of six new regional offices and new facilities, and the challenges coming from emerging competitors they hadn't faced before.

Before I was even offered the position, I started reading everything I could find about the company: the strategic plan, corporate messages about focus and expectations, whatever was posted on the corporate website, and myriad other strategic documents and papers.

I learned quickly that the company had created a mountain of documentation that looked like it had been written by fifteen different writers with competing ideas. The documents and messages didn't mesh, resulting in hundreds of pages of contradictory content. I happened to know that the company had, over the previous year or two, crafted an exciting new message that expressed its new approach to the customer. But the new message was totally missing from its plans. Early on I met with Peter, a colleague whom I had bonded with quickly, and I told him that I didn't have the slightest idea what we were trying to tell our people or the marketplace. The website didn't agree with the strategic plan. The critical messages were lost in the countless documents. And, worst of all, when I spoke with different people, I got completely different interpretations about the business focus and the messages that the company was sending to the employees and the marketplace.

Everybody was working, and not everyone was clueless; but in terms of working toward achieving the company goals, almost everyone was off track—pointing in wrong directions ranging from slight to severe. You couldn't find a single employee who didn't need to shift his workload, change tasks, reevaluate timetables, or realign priorities to get back in line.

My first initiative was to spearhead a project to start over and get a new strategic plan in the hands of every employee within thirty days. How could I affect operations without a clear purpose for our work?

This story illustrates how crucial it is that companies focus on all three elements—strategy, alignment, and execution—if they want to function as effective and exceptional companies.

What to Know About Path 7

Many companies have spent lots of time on developing a strategy and strategic planning. Most companies spend much more time on their strategic plan than alignment and execution combined. But strategy should have a short journey from ideas to development to communication—short enough that it quickly becomes part of the daily work of all employees. That is seldom true. Unfortunately, the journey is usually long and painful and often stops short. Strategy is the map that every employee needs for directions. Teams cannot get to the end of the road without clear messages, clear expectations, and clear action plans.

Companies need to plan carefully how to disseminate their strategy to their employees. Strategic planning is too often the work of the key leaders, who then expect their plan to reach everyone in the company—often by itself—which, of course, does not happen. High-performing companies set up the processes for sharing, integrating, and executing strategy. Without those processes, leaders will be out of sync, managers at the next level will be out of sync, and strategy will be ignored, creating a cascade of fake work from top to bottom. Everyone will be aiming at the wrong target. This is how a company falls behind the competition. This is how companies fail.

Eleven Strategic-Planning Problems That Cause Fake Work

The following problems often occur during the development and implementation of a strategic plan:

1. **Being passive about the process.** Strategic planning should be a serious and critical focus of every company. But some companies, especially new and smaller ones, assume that talking

about strategy is enough. Or they may not take time for strategic thinking at all. Or they don't make any real effort to spread it through the company.

2. **Taking too much time to develop and write strategies and far too long for the whole process.** We worked with a company that had a great idea that took *five years* to go from an idea to a strategic plan to action items to actually bringing the idea to their employees. Originally, that great idea would have put them out in front of their competition. But by the time they acted on it, they were merely in pace with many of their competitors. Once a strategy is developed, there are many steps to getting it to all employees. Very often that process is unnecessarily arduous, careless, and very lengthy, even endless.

3. **Not formalizing the strategic plan.** Strategy isn't an idea—it is a series of choices about how you are presenting yourself in the marketplace, how you focus the business, how you respond to changes. It takes time to formulate and take root. It requires commitment and attention. It must be written, published, and shared. It demands a process for rolling it out that is well thought out and effective. The problem is that companies focus on creating the strategy but do very little to get the strategy to their employees in an easily understood and useful manner.

4. **Failing to develop first-rate strategic documents.** If the strategic plan is not well written and well articulated, it is essentially useless. Many leaders like their strategic plans at the idea stage, but when the idea is expressed in a corporate document the writing is often mediocre, frequently confusing, sometimes impenetrable, and occasionally too complex for most readers.

5. **Keeping employees at a distance.** Management often acts as if developing strategy is some big secret project, and does not involve employees in the process. Ultimately, the company needs lots of input to ensure that the strategies make sense and are realistic, and it needs to get employees interested and en-

thusiastic, which occurs when the employees feel they have played a role in its creation.

6. **Failing to sell or promote the benefits of strategy.** If employees aren't given clear reasons to get on board and get excited—or to at least understand the benefits of the plan— they will not help drive strategies forward. The last thing a company needs is apathy, and apathy is best combated with good plans that will ultimately benefit everyone.

7. **Failing to translate the strategic plan into actual work.** Strategies must be understood and turned into tasks that can be put to work to get results. Leaders must have a plan to help employees translate their daily work tasks into critical tasks that focus on the strategic plan. Too often it is assumed that this will happen, but it does not happen without a well-devised framework in place.

8. **Not requesting and responding to feedback.** A serious problem often happens when the strategies hit the point of work. They don't make sense, they don't work, customers react negatively, and there is misunderstanding about how the strategy applies to the actual work an employee does. The strategic process demands a concerted effort to listen for and request feedback on the effectiveness of the plan. When companies get a plan out quickly and seek input quickly, they can quickly make adjustments to the plan or to their communication of the plan.

9. **Failing to execute strategy.** Without execution a strategic plan is just words on paper. Companies spend millions of dollars to develop strategies, send them out, and sometimes even work with managers on the meaning and on methods for disseminating the strategic documents, but then they do little if anything to see the strategy put to work: There's no follow-up, no retooling, no honing, no coaching, no execution—resulting in much fake work.

10. **Not managing the process or rewarding execution.** All strategic work needs to be managed by individuals and/or managers. It also needs to be rewarded. Unfortunately, companies tend to reward executives simply for developing strategies—often whether they're successful or not—but they rarely find ways to show appreciation for the people who execute the strategy.

11. **Failing to measure the execution of strategy.** Execution is about precision—about doing the work itself as effectively as possible. All critical work tasks need to have quantifiable measures of success attached to them. As Peter Drucker said, "What gets measured gets done."

Alignment Brings People Together to Work on the Right Stuff

We were boarding a plane one day and looked in the cockpit. The pilot, the copilot, and the navigator were going through their checklists. When we got to our seats, we considered the question: "What if they aren't exactly on the same page?" Our conversation led us to examine the consequences of a misaligned team. What if we had passed by and heard:

"I thought you were going to do that."

"That's not my job."

"I think I checked that already."

"I don't know, is that important?"

Flying can be nerve-racking enough without passengers seeing signs of a flight team confused about their roles and responsibilities. Luckily, our crew seemed to be aligned—they knew what they needed to do, understood the difference in their roles, and were working together, seamlessly, to execute their tasks—in this case, getting a plane in the air and back on the ground safely.

And alignment wasn't just happening in the cockpit. Off the plane as well, pilots periodically discuss issues and how to rethink and retool their work, explore the gaps in their learning, or share problems that they should all prepare for and know how to avoid.

Alignment is continuous. It is an interdependent exercise to bring people together to do the best work in the most efficient way possible. It is about knowing yourself and your team so well that you can constantly improve precision.

Execution Is, Simply, Doing the Work Itself

If alignment is illustrated by the pilots and navigator in the cockpit, then execution is the work itself—the takeoff, the flight, and the landing. Teams that are well aligned are prepared to execute.

Execution is work that is done precisely, work that is targeted to the right issues and is honed to get the best results. Like alignment, execution is also an ongoing process. It takes time and has to be adjusted constantly. If it isn't updated, to employ the pilot analogy one last time, the company will be off course and miss the runway.

As we mentioned earlier, companies often make the mistake of spending a large amount of their time on developing a strategy, then drop the ball when it comes to alignment and execution. In fact, many companies fall into the 80–20 trap—they spend about 80 percent of their effort developing and refining strategy but only 20 percent aligning and executing. The assumption, too often, is that work is work. As long as people are busy, people assume that real work is occurring. By now, you know that all work is not equal. Execution is the place where you prove that. And great efforts from strategy should not be left to die at the point of work—turning all the work that went into formulating the strategy into fake work.

Strategic planning will not succeed unless employees know what their company's strategy means, and understand the benefits of the changes and the implications of the changes for them and their work. Alignment is critical work but not if companies aren't ready to execute—to get the work done with precision, on time, with excellence. And execution is not just the intent, but the actual work; not the effort, but the finish line. The following steps will help bring together the three key elements of strategy, alignment, and execution.

Steps to Move Down Path 7

Step 1: Make Your Strategic Planning and Implementation Process Real

Strategy is how a company plans to drive its mission, vision, values, and objectives into the work itself. Mission, vision, and values—and even high-level objectives or goals—are meant to be stable and generally should not change much, if at all, from year to year. Strategy is where the company determines shifts in emphasis and ideas and provides the energy and opportunity to head in different directions.

Strategies are meant to respond to customer needs, employee concerns, or market forces. Sometimes they change and help companies survive or blossom; certainly that is the expectation. But often strategies cause a tsunami through the company and have difficulty being aligned or executed, and leave wreckage in the aftermath.

CUTTING COSTS, CUTTING SALES

A big chain of electronics stores recently decided to cut costs by firing everyone on the floor who made over $8 an hour. It was a remarkably stupid idea, and devastating, because it took knowledgeable and experienced people out of the workforce. Customers immediately understood that they wouldn't find skilled people to help them. Managers found they were working with the youngest and least experienced employees. Sales plummeted. The chain ended up hiring, or trying to hire, many people back, but it may not survive this terrible decision.

Most likely, the electronics chain did not have a strategy at all, but only a reactionary plan for cost-cutting. When formal processes are not in place—with clear decisions made with quality data—informal systems take over. It doesn't feel strategic, but the shortsighted cost-cutting measure was an informal strategy.

As the story illustrated, companies need to ensure they have and use strategy and follow it and measure it and improve it over time. In addition, companies need to keep the "big picture" in mind—in the instance of the electronics chain, the company panicked and chose an unwise cost-cutting measure that, had they looked at the overall situation, they obviously shouldn't have implemented. Clearly, the company's sales were one of its biggest assets, and the company threw those assets away. This story also demonstrates the importance of knowing your people: Where people are doing vital work without knowledge, strategies are just pipe dreams.

Step 2: Create and Articulate Strategies That Can Be Turned into Work

A significant weakness for many strategic development teams is that they fail to articulate and translate strategy in terms that the entire organization can understand, rely upon, and—most important—execute.

A strategic plan is a formal document that defines, explains, and illuminates strategies for all employees. To be effective, these strategic plans must:

1. Be well written—as short and concise as possible, but with enough detail to help all readers understand the focus and the calls to action.
2. Provide a clear link to the elements of strategy, such as the mission, vision, and objectives.
3. Provide context so that readers understand company history, market influences, or other elements that they will need to read and understand the plan.
4. Sell or promote the benefits to the readers and the benefits to the company.
5. Explain the implications of the changes. Give specific examples, perhaps in several areas.
6. Provide the reasoning for changes.

7. Lay out strategies and measures of success wherever possible.
8. Be reviewed by a broad sampling of readers across the company to check for clarity and effectiveness.

The following story indicates how misinterpretation can derail big, potentially business-saving plans.

DOES THIS STRATEGY CHANGE ANYTHING?

My manager, Louie, was the first to tell us about the new strategies. He said our strategy had changed from selling our engines to focusing more on the maintenance of the engines. Louie added he didn't think the new strategy changed anything because we would go on working with our clients as we always had. Then I read the strategy document that Louie provided. It seemed to me that the changes were huge. So I suggested that our team have a meeting with Tricia, our COO, to see if she could shed some light on all the potential changes.

We all met and Tricia explained that we were adjusting our whole business model, sales model, pricing model, contracting process, and the way we talked to and worked with clients. She talked about how the strategy would be phased in and about our role in operations. That meeting helped me and our team to see how we should examine all our tasks and our priorities to see how we would adjust to the new strategy—it was invaluable.

Hundreds of workers could have been working against the company's new strategies because of one person's misinterpretation of them. We've found that the real distinction of an excellent company is its ability to articulate and translate its strategies in terms that people can actually understand and in ways that allow people to apply them to what they do on a day-to-day basis.

Step 3: Communicate Company Strategies Effectively to Employees

Strategy has to be sold. It has to leave the thinkers' and writers' hands and get into the hands of managers and teams where most of the work happens. Too often the whole process is too long and poorly implemented. The goal is to avoid making fake work of the strategy development phase by getting strategy out quickly and effectively, and this is where communication comes into play. Here are some simple guidelines for communicating company strategy:

- Create a communication plan that defines goals for the plan, the types of communication needed, the purpose of each different type, and the communication methods.
- Communicate quickly. Get the messages out as soon as possible.
- Communicate in many different ways: formal documents sent to everyone, e-mails, Internet links to the documents, conference calls, etc.
- Plan for additional levels of communication that are more personal—like one-on-one meetings with teams and their managers. Create support materials to help managers translate the strategy correctly.
- Don't just speak, listen. Communication requires feedback so you can be sure that the message is being understood.
- Follow up. Then follow up again. Listen carefully and gather information that will help leaders understand problems and concerns with implementation.

The following story by Pablo illustrates the problems that result from delays and breakdowns in communication.

THE GREEN PAGES

I worked for a large company that had hired me to address communication issues and to facilitate getting key messages to employees (the company seemed to have a lot of breakdowns in which messages they sent out didn't seem to reach a large percentage of people). Working with the company's communication committee, I discovered that a major communication vehicle was its newsletter, *The Green Pages*, of which its members were very proud.

I read about thirty past issues of *The Green Pages*, as well as the current one, which included some very important information about benefits adjustments. The newsletter was distributed to all employees, so the committee thought it was effectively getting out information to everyone in the company. I thought some of the writing was good, but overall I found the newsletters boring and cluttered. They also mixed information and other content poorly, so that things got lost—they just weren't designed well.

Knowing the CEO liked the newsletter, I went to the company's corporate office building and watched as several people handed out the newsletters in the morning, at lunch, and at closing time. I watched people take them and drop them in nearby garbage cans without even reading them. I interviewed about twenty-five employees to find out why they weren't bothering to read the newsletter, and the response was almost always the same: "It never says anything that matters to me." When I pointed out the benefits article, they were a little surprised. Most of them took the newsletter back from me to give it another look.

I took pictures. I retrieved newsletters from the garbage cans, piles of them, and brought them back to the communication team. We started a new discussion about the cost of all the work that was ending up in the trash and brainstormed new ways to deliver important messages to employees.

Situations like the one above happen all the time, and they can be devastating to companies that try to disseminate strategic plans using similar methods.

Step 4: Close the Execution Gap

We call misalignment the "execution gap," which is the chasm between strategy and work. The gap is wider than many think because most people simply don't understand how essential alignment is to the strategic process.

To close the execution gap, executives, managers, and other leaders must start aligning with each other. They must each understand their most critical tasks—the work that is most essential to drive strategy into the organization. Too often, executives are buried under dozens of tasks that pull them off center. That is the first sign of a breakdown. Then, they must work to integrate their work with each other—basically walking through the team alignment process in Path 6. Finally, they have to ensure that the process cascades through the company and that at each level people take ownership of the process. The goal is to get the strategic plan out of the executive offices and onto every employee's critical task list.

The Fallacy of Managers Aligning Their Teams

The biggest alignment mistake companies suffer is when managers think they can align their teams on their own—one employee at a time. This is a fallacy. Alignment is more art than science. Unfortunately, the whole idea is often relegated to performance reviews during which managers sit with employees and try to adjust them—align them if possible—to the needs of the company and the team. With a car, this may work: Slowly and surely you can keep turning screws and tightening bolts until the tires are aligned. With human beings, however, alignment requires collaboration, communication, and subtle adjustments with our teams. The art of aligning people lies in listening and understanding and adapting their personal needs to those of the team and the company.

The process should entail people working together to discover the best ways to achieve goals and to adjust to new situations. Company leaders at every level must ensure that alignment will happen by:

1. Encouraging open and honest discussion.
2. Investing in alignment sessions, in which people work at understanding their roles and their teammates' roles in collectively accomplishing critical work.
3. Ensuring that all team members know what all the others do and how it affects their work.
4. Having managers and their teams create critical tasks together and agree on priorities and value.
5. Getting rid of fake work, and getting rid of low-priority items that take the team's focus away from critical tasks.
6. Rewarding teams for working extremely well together toward achieving company goals.

Step 5: Do the Work Itself with Precision, and Measure It

Execution is all about doing the right work. Analyzing the work you do, and constantly working to make sure it's what you should be doing, will ensure your company success and reduce your fake work output even further.

Here are some key ways to avoid fake work and enable people to execute with excellence:

- **Know the work.** If you are a leader, you must know the work that your team does. You must get involved, get dirty, and get real. Nothing hurts execution more than unrealistic strategy.
- **Determine which tasks are critical.** Critical tasks are the few tasks that focus most directly on the company's most important efforts. For example, a task might be to do maintenance checks on a bottling line. A critical task might be to revise and upgrade the maintenance schedule to reduce downtime by 10 percent.
- **Establish clear expectations for projects and programs.** Establish milestones and deadlines, deliverables and outputs for all projects and tasks where possible to provide a way to analyze efficiencies, troubleshoot problems, and improve the processes over time.

- **Take ownership of the challenges and opportunities.** Real work is not just thinking or strategizing—it is action. It is the focal point of value. Doing real work makes the whole process and all the people in it feel more valuable.
- **Communicate back through the system.** Once you've identified the best practices, you need to push that information into the communication channels to ensure that they are noticed and implemented by the entire company.
- **Establish metrics for all work.** At every level of the company, metrics need to be in place to measure the effectiveness of work. The more quantifiable the data, the better.
- **Work with your team.** Simply put, in the modern workplace you need each other to execute. So work with your team to improve results, but also to reduce distractions and to decrease problems. Efficient teamwork is highly satisfying work.
- **Build in rewards that propagate real work.** Rewards are often out of whack. Many rewards happen at top levels, while few rewards, other than paychecks, happen at the bottom—where all the work is executed. Rewards need to include reinforcement, recognition, and empowerment, so people can achieve the rich reward of work well done, as well as monetary rewards. Reward only the real work that is driving the business forward, not fake work.

While all of these above suggestions serve the company and may help improve the effectiveness of managers, they are critical to every employee's effectiveness and job satisfaction.

A Roadmap for Action

Ask yourself the following questions:

- Does your company have a strategic planning process and is it transparent?

- How would you describe your company's strategic planning and implementation process? Is it effective? Does it use company resources effectively?

- Does your process involve careful development, precise articulation, and excellent documents and presentations to ensure clarity and understanding?

- Have you introduced a formal communication plan to ensure that information gets out, gets read, and gets the attention it deserves?

- Does your process involve steps to translate strategic intent—to help managers and employees at all levels understand strategies and the implications of any changes and any benefits to the company and to employees?

- Are you engaging in alignment steps with your team to clarify work, to discover overlaps and gaps, to prioritize, and to prepare to execute?

- Have you focused attention on execution as well as strategy so that work is launched, observed, measured, and rewarded?

- Are people sharing problems with managers that percolate back to the top?

- Are your teams sharing best practices to repeat great work over and over again?

- What conditions in the workplace are particularly distracting to you and your team? How can you mitigate the negative effects on your work?

PATH 8
Managing Real Work

People leave managers, not companies.
— *Marcus Buckingham and Curt Coffman*

PATH 8 IS about the critical role managers play in the workplace. It is about the very difficult job of being a manager and how this role is crucial in eradicating fake work in companies. Managers play a pivotal role in either facilitating real work or enabling fake work.

A common definition of a manager, no matter the level, is one who works with and through others to achieve company results. In other words, the role of the manager is to turn strategic intent into real work. It is critical that managers understand and address fake work in their teams and in their own actions. The ways managers must approach work with their employees, if they are to help build high-performance teams, include:

- Focusing on the work that actually needs to be done.
- Understanding company strategies and the team's relationship to each strategy.
- Being a conduit of information to each team member regarding the company's strategies.
- Translating company strategies into specific critical tasks that can be executed by each team member to help drive company results.
- Empowering team members so they take responsibility for communicating, solving problems, making decisions, and sharing information.
- Accounting for and following up with each team member to make certain that the critical tasks are completed.

If managers and their teams understand their relationship, and if managers ensure that they are helping employees do real work—rather than acting as impediments—then it is very difficult for teams to do fake work. At the same time, individuals in a work team must learn to work with and understand their managers, and managers must share in the responsibility for making that happen. In this path, we will address the following steps toward improving your abilities as a manager and toward helping you and your team execute real work.

Step 1: Change your management behaviors.
Step 2: Translate strategies to facilitate real work.
Step 3: Manage performance through alignment.
Step 4: Remove the barriers to real work.
Step 5: Set up monitoring systems and share success.

Path 8 is important because the management role is critical to the completion of real work. Companies need managers as points of accountability, and they need managers to carry the mission of the company to their work teams—and then help to implement it.

Being an effective manager requires managing people and processes as well as exhibiting leadership skills such as interpersonal communication, collaboration, mentoring, and coaching skills. Management also involves skills such as monitoring, collecting data, measuring success, and providing detailed analysis to help make decisions and solve problems.

If either managers or their employees—or, worse, both—misunderstand the functions of the management role, serious problems in the workplace will arise, such as a breakdown in communication, misdirected work, and failure to get results.

Harold's story illustrates the important role that efficient managers can play in more effectively getting work done.

MANAGING THE HUB AND SPOKES OF CHAOS

My company has hundreds of construction projects going on at any one time—industrial buildings, complexes, houses, large developments, etc. For years we had a traditional hub-and-spokes model for how we managed all our projects: If we had a development site where, for example, we were building thirty-five houses, we would assign a project director to that project to oversee the site. Each project involved many other managers and supervisors, but the director was the center-piece, or hub, for the project. Our project directors worked mostly in the corporate office, where they maintained constant contact with all the contractors and subcontractors—the spokes—out in the field.

Every day on our sites, hundreds of tasks were taking place at projects in varying stages of development. While one hous-ing site was being excavated, at another site plumbing pipes were being laid; at another the foundations were being poured; the next was being framed; at the next someone was doing electrical work; at the next kitchens were being built; then someone was painting; and so on to all the finish work to close a project and have a house ready to sell. Different contractors and subcontractors handled all of those tasks, and every time a problem popped up, it went into the hub. If the folks laying the pipe had problems with the excavation, they called the project director. One of our directors, Reggie, said he was handling up to a hundred calls a day about all kinds of issues. The problems could be as serious as electrical wiring done improperly or as mundane as dirt left in the foundation that the plumbing guys had to move before they went to work.

You can imagine the conflicts and anger that could crop up on the sites at any time. Some level of conflict was happening dozens of times a day—and it was all passed on to Reggie. Reggie would take a call from the plumbers, then call the foun-dation people, then call the plumbers back, and so on—all day long. Reggie was the control center for every problem, but he described his office as the "out-of-control center." He didn't have time to breathe. One day Reggie was in a car accident that laid him up for five days. He spent the majority of his rehabilitation thinking about how he didn't want to go back to work.

Then he realized that our company's entire model was built on the idea of central control, to give the company control over the contractors. Reggie realized that he shouldn't have to manage or be the go-between for these various people. They were all able and smart professionals.

So he, along with a team that included representatives from the contractors, redesigned the process. They set up a system in which the contractors talked directly to each other and worked through their problems. Then they set up agreements among all the contractors that defined expectations for entering and leaving the site, agreed on completion checklists, etc. Reggie's new approach put almost all the burden on the people on the sites to solve problems and work together, to align, and to build relationships.

Reggie became a coordinator and a partner with the contractors, and the amount of real work increased. There was plenty to do, but it was all productive and valuable work. He got to mentor others, improve relations between teams, and train field managers and contractors to help everyone succeed.

This story illustrates that management can be done in many different ways, and it highlights the effectiveness of a manager who aligns workers with one another.

What to Know About Path 8

To reduce fake work, managers must assess, address, and solve mismanagement issues that creep into their teams. Managers live in a difficult place: They are often caught between their bosses and their work teams, so they have demands above and below them. Not only are they caught, but they are being pulled in many directions. Given that tension and the competing demands most managers face, it's no wonder that we hear so many comments like these:

- "My boss is a bureaucrat. She loves to make sure that everyone is loaded down with useless paperwork. She had to do it before she was a manager, so now we have to do it, too."
- "My supervisor is a dictator. He learned his management skills in the military. He can't talk; he bellows. He doesn't listen. He blames, he punishes."
- "Our project manager is useless. She never makes a decision. She hates and avoids all conflicts."
- "Our manager is very creative, but he's entirely out of touch with reality."
- "My team leader never communicates anything but he thinks he does, which is very frustrating. He actually has no idea what communication is and how he could be more helpful."

Consider the issues that affect work—and cause fake work—and try to determine whether your company is being affected by any of the management problems we detail below.

Eleven Mismanagement Issues That Lead to Fake Work

1. **Looking at work from thirty thousand feet will not get real work done on the ground.** Managers, especially in upper management, often spend too much time looking at the organization from 30,000 feet—high up in the executive offices with no sense of the details—and spend too little time on the ground communicating with those who don't get to fly so high. The managers don't understand employees' work and therefore aren't in a position to understand or solve problems, to address the barriers that stand in a worker's way, or discuss performance with any real knowledge.

2. **Management and micromanagement are not the same thing.** When micromanagers check up on and insert themselves into every task, employees feel like children. Micromanagers even-

tually end up taking over the work while the team simply yields to them. It hurts loyalty, trust, and respect.

3. **If you do it, they will let you.** If you insist on doing, reviewing, or redoing tasks, your employees will do less and less, or cease doing tasks altogether, assuming that you will revise their work anyway. This is an extremely important concept. Managers, like the micromanagers above, often rewrite reports, fix e-mails, critique behaviors, and review everything. Ultimately, this makes employees feel disempowered and disrespected. Managers do need to provide guidance and coaching, but if they take over projects or tasks, employees will find ways to reduce their work and allow managers to do more of it.

4. **Failing to understand strategy will disarm teams.** Often managers don't understand strategy and they don't understand their role in implementing strategies. They become the barrier between the critical goals of the company and the work the team could do to make those goals real—the precise opposite of what a manager should be. For example, at the project level, managers seldom link their projects to the strategies of the company.

5. **Not clarifying and translating strategies into work hurts alignment and execution.** Without a manager learning about, understanding, communicating, and translating strategies into tasks, teams can't align their tasks to strategies and do real work.

6. **Trying to align employees will end up as fake work.** Managers believe that they can align their teams but they can't. Alignment is a people task between individuals on a work team. Managers have to get involved but must not interfere with the process. Teams will align themselves if their manager adequately explains strategies and helps prioritize and align critical tasks.

7. **Bureaucratic behavior seldom serves the team or the company.** Often managers set up illusions of work. They delegate

and demand repetitive, useless tasks that follow the patterns of businesses dating to the start of the Industrial Revolution. It is pure fake work that creates huge deficits in employee commitment and care. It steals time and effort from the real work that employees should be doing in the first place.

8. **Delegating fake work causes confusion and conflict.** Often managers come up with off-the-cuff ideas that they insert blithely into work processes, rather than thoughtfully aligning them with a strategic plan. Their employees get whiplash as they try to stay abreast of the latest directive. Then those same managers seem surprised when their teams are never really on track.

9. **Rewarding fake work creates a chasm between managers and their teams that is hard to close up.** Rewards are very important in the workplace. Rewards include promotions, bonuses, and certificates, but more important, they include public comments, special privileges, and kind words. Anytime a manager rewards an employee for doing fake work—even in the subtlest way—it propagates a system of fake-work behaviors that becomes ingrained in the workplace. It affects teamwork and confidence in the manager and skepticism about real work and its value.

10. **Managing performance through traditional review systems enables fake work.** We like to call typical performance review processes "systems of surprise." Under this approach, managers don't set expectations, communicate, provide feedback, monitor results, or respond to variances any time but in a meeting a couple of times a year in performance reviews. And then, in those reviews, employees get hit with the surprise. Sometimes the surprise is that the manager has no idea what the employee has been doing. Sometimes it's that the manager is disappointed with the employee's work although they agreed on the priorities. Sometimes managers ignore results and accomplishments, but have remarkable memory for the smallest problem or disappointment. These systems often distort reality and seriously impair the work of individuals and teams.

11. **Failing to remove barriers and advocate for employees will hurt performance.** The workplace is mired in procedures and policies that are simply barriers to real work. Managers who don't help rid their teams of these intruding tasks, processes, and bureaucratic policies will deal instead with unmotivated, unfocused workers—and of course, lagging results.

Employees Must Understand Their Relationship with Their Manager

Managers are critical to the success of any company, but every employee has an opportunity to affect the quality and value that each manager brings to the table. Regardless of your role, your manager is a part of your team. Rightly, companies put a lot of responsibility on managers, but that doesn't mean employees should use managers as an excuse for poor performance.

Rather than focusing so much on your manager's shortcomings, consider your own role and invoke the Golden Rule: Treat your manager the way you would like to be treated. Rethink your responsibility in the management relationship. Just as you need your manager to make decisions and solve problems that affect you and your work, your manager needs a good, open relationship with every member of the team. Your basic responsibilities to your manager include providing feedback, problem-solving, communicating, and learning as much as possible to help your team and your manager succeed.

The work environment is organic and dynamic. It requires sensitivity, adaptation, and responsiveness from both managers and team members. We heard the following entertaining story, which illustrates how managers must respond with creativity and innovation to the challenges that will inevitably come at them.

MANAGING MONKEY GOLF

Managers at a golf course in Asia faced an unusual situation: The course was inundated with monkeys—creative, pesky, delightful monkeys. The monkeys loved to pick up golf balls and move them around—into the grasses, the trees, the bushes, and the lakes. The golfers didn't find that delightful at all! The managers did everything they could think of to ward off or divert the monkeys, but nothing worked. The frustrated golfers knew there wasn't another course in the area.

Finally, the managers and the golfers teamed up to produce a solution: They created a rule called "play it where the monkey drops it." While it took some time to accept and adapt to the randomness of the new game, the golfers eventually began to embrace its special challenges. In fact, once word got out, other golfers came from great distances to try their luck against the monkeys on the newly famous course.

This story is funny on the surface and remarkably interesting as you look deeper. It shows how effective management responds to the realities in front of them, not their preconceived notions. While challenges in a workplace may not be as crazy as monkey golf, they often require just as creative and flexible a solution. Managers must adapt to circumstances, but they must also help their employees prepare for change and adaptation. The only thing that doesn't change is the fact that things do change. Managers often get stuck trying to make old models work under remarkably new circumstances. How much more success the golf course managers achieved by thinking in a new way.

Steps to Move Down Path 8

Step 1: Change Your Management Behaviors

To achieve results and do real work, most managers will need to adopt at least some new behaviors. Below is a list of ideas you should consider as you prepare to fight fake work, in addition to all of the behaviors we've covered throughout the book that will help you be an effective and valued employee.

- **Model company values—and understand them.** Use them to navigate your own behaviors and model the behaviors you want and need in others. Begin by being the best person you can be in light of your company's values before you demand the same from others.

- **Communicate and help others communicate with each other.** A manager's very first job is to communicate. Managers are the conduits for information coming from the top, translators of information, facilitators of change—in other words, communicators. Then each manager must set up the conditions for others to feel safe to communicate, and must set expectations for clear and consistent communication among team members.

- **Coach, mentor, and guide people to do the work required to be successful.** If you coach, mentor, and guide your fellow workers, they will usually appreciate it and work harder and more effectively. Being a coach takes time, but the payoff is very large. And there's an added benefit: The better you coach and mentor, the less you will have to do it in the future because employees don't want to leave managers who empower them, trust them, and take pride in their success.

- **Participate and stay involved.** You can't play the game looking through the window.

- **Empower your team by delegating real work.** Make sure you're providing your employees with valuable work to do—and then trust them to do it.

- **Look for the good things that are happening and mention them—specifically and respectfully.** Don't police the perimeter either looking for mistakes or dropping by with "attaboys." Neither is perceived as positive feedback in the workplace.

- **Advocate for your people and your teams.** You will be rewarded for your courage if you champion those who work for you. Show the organization how much you respect and care for your people.

- **Seek out and hire people with the competencies that will serve the critical work that needs to be done.** Don't just look at a résumé. Skills and talents that look good on paper may have nothing to do with your need for people who excel at teamwork or customer service.

If you, as a manager, exhibit the above behaviors, your employees will live and act in an environment of real work. This will make it easier for you, your team, and your employees to become partners and active participants in aligning work with your company's strategies.

Even if you're not a manager, everything on the above list of behaviors will help you be more successful in your job. For example, just because you don't manage doesn't mean you should not mentor or coach coworkers. We can all be advocates for those with whom we work.

Step 2: Translate Strategies to Facilitate Real Work

Everyone in a company should know its mission, vision, and values. The objectives and high-level goals of the company give you your measures of success. While everyone should be aware of strategy, managers must be the ears of the team and pay close attention to the messages of the company that relate to its strategies, initiatives, and priorities because they shift and change often—perhaps too often. Managers must transfer the key messages of the company to their teams and aid in the process of alignment.

Step 3: Manage Performance Through Alignment and Review Your Employees Accordingly

Once teams are aligned, they should have critical tasks that are prioritized, have clear deliverables and timelines, and measures of success. That is everything a manager needs to review and discuss performance.

Far too often, traditional performance management processes may be fake work from start to finish. These performance review processes thwart the simplicity of discussing work as a team by putting managers and employees in rooms one on one to have private conversations that derail alignment and hamper execution, rather than in groups where employees talk and solve problems. While traditional review processes are better than nothing at all, a peer process is a much better way to create effective and cohesive teams and to build responsibility for actions.

However, managers have to understand that they can't mandate performance. What they can do is support, coach, mentor, and build conditions for performance, which are critical if a company is going to be successful.

Consider the example of Martin, who owns a small retail manufacturing plant that imports, among other things, handmade cloth from India and transforms it into napkins, table runners, and other specialty domestic items.

ETHNIC CHIC

Martin's company had been meeting its basic goals for growth and revenue for several years running, but the company had never really taken off in the way he thought it could. Even though the market had seen a dramatic surge in interest in "ethnic chic" products, Martin's business hadn't grown and he was worried that it wouldn't be able to survive if it didn't increase its sales. The demand was there, so the problem was clearly with supply.

Martin wanted to grow sales by at least 10 percent, and he hired a couple of consultants to help assess the problem. After surveying the organization, the consultants suggested instituting a performance management system that would help Martin weed out the slower workers, improve productivity, and reward the star performers.

The company relied on a lot of local part-time labor. Many of the workers were stay-at-home moms who took piecework home with them and worked on it at night or during their children's naptime. The consultants encouraged Martin to let these folks go and to hire a core staff of five full-time employees who would work on site. But Martin was reluctant to lay off so many of his community-based moms. He told the consultants he'd think about their recommendations.

Then he called a meeting for his employees to see what

they thought of the recommendations. He told them that whatever they said would be fine—he was just interested in hearing how things were really working out on the front lines and if they thought the consultants' recommendations would do any good.

One employee, Mary, told him that she often got her cutouts done ahead of time but had to wait days for the edgers to complete the finishing work. Only then could she finish the item by attaching the special fringe that was too delicate to be handled by the big machines.

Kyson, an edger, said she was constantly overwhelmed by the people who did cutouts because they would drop off a huge batch and expect them to be done by the end of the day. If she could just establish a rough schedule, she could give them a more accurate timeline and wouldn't have to edge all the items at once.

Dorothy, a finish worker, reported that she felt redundant because she never had enough work to do. She said she'd rather be an edger so that she could actually do some real work instead of sitting around all day long.

The conversation continued all day, and every employee had at least one concrete suggestion to improve the overall process. The more the group talked, the more they realized that their problems were not productivity- or morale-related, but were simply workflow hiccups—alignment problems.

They didn't need a complex performance management system—what they really needed was a clear conversation about how work happened in their company. The consultants' solutions focused only on processes and procedures, but their employees' straightforward work discussion had focused them on why people were doing what they were doing and how that affected what they were doing.

Martin inadvertently stumbled upon alignment and found that it was a more valuable way to assess performance and performance issues than any performance management process could have been. This is often the case. If you and your employees can align performance through the lens of the team, your productivity levels will rise just as Martin's did.

Manager Difficulties Using Performance Management Systems

Managers often become victims of a performance management process that gets in the way of effective relations with teams and team members in the following ways:

- **Managers don't talk about anything relevant or important in review meetings.** They don't talk about expectations, measures of success, or priorities of work; instead they talk about a specific task or an error on a report. Employees leave feeling confused and disconnected.
- **Managers ignore the tough issues—even when the review is a private meeting and the logical time to discuss an employee's weaknesses.** Research shows that a very big complaint against managers and supervisors is their unwillingness to discuss negative issues and concerns. They wait until something pushes it over the edge.
- **Managers bring up failures that employees are totally unaware of.** Often managers wait until a review to bring up an employee's past mistakes, like a bad presentation or a missed project milestone. Of course these discussions should have happened when they occurred so employees could understand the issues, relate to them, and adjust and solve problems. It does no good to chastise an employee for a mistake four or six months later.
- **Managers are passive-aggressive and make a dramatic shift in their behavior from the workplace to the one-on-one review.** Some managers think the quiet of their office is a place to unleash on an employee whom they have ignored or failed to communicate with for months.
- **Managers aren't asking for feedback.** Some managers don't listen for or request feedback at all. Some use a performance

review as the only time to ask for feedback, ignoring every other opportunity to get feedback or clarify issues about work priorities and expectations in a timely manner.

- **Managers use the review period for rewards, but they are like private deals that aren't fair or just.** Because each review is private and because managers are often naive or forgetful about real work and real value, the reward process isn't any better. It is full of favoritism, bias, and carelessness. And it gets worse when, inevitably, employees talk and they discover the discrepancies. Managers who assumed they were in a private conversation now have to deal with anger and hurt regarding unfair practices and unjust treatment. These employee concerns can destroy a team and create tons of fake work.

Now that we've pointed out the negatives to avoid, we'll give you some tips for managing performance the right way—through alignment. Setting expectations, giving and receiving feedback, monitoring performance, and working with and aligning teams all work much better in a team environment, as in the alignment model that follows, than in individual performance reviews.

Manage Performance Through an Alignment Model

We would never suggest a company throw out its entire performance management process because it likely has some elements that should be retained. However, you should consider adjusting your performance management process to work through an alignment model. To do that:

- Discuss the key elements of performance reviews in a very public, very open meeting with your teams.
- Set expectations.
- Define critical tasks.
- Prioritize critical tasks.
- Determine measures of success—deadlines, budgets, deliverables, and expected results.

- Have open and honest communication, with your employees focused on real work.
- Adjust and align all the work of each team member to the strategies of the company.
- Meet and agree on critical work tasks with managers.
- Ensure that everyone knows what critical tasks everyone else is doing.
- Motivate team members to execute and to get work done with excellence.
- Monitor through the teams. Let team members monitor and report on their effectiveness and check for compliance to agreements.
- Follow up over and over again.

Step 4: Remove the Barriers to Real Work

As a manager, you must do everything possible to remove barriers that separate people from the real work they need to do. You can easily keep people busy, but you must keep the road clear for real and valuable work. The workplace is a minefield—loaded with interruptions, setbacks, policies, processes, and procedures—but managers must work to clear all of those barriers that don't support real work. Some common barriers include:

- Policies and practices that are too restrictive or don't add value.
- Redundant or useless steps in processes.
- Meetings that don't have a very clear purpose.
- Meetings that pull people in just to be observers.
- Conference calls, videoconferences, etc., that have no clear purpose.

Step 5: Set Up Monitoring Systems and Share Success

Make sure you are setting up ways to follow up, check in, and monitor work without being unduly intrusive. The best way to do that is to hold employees accountable and expect them to measure and to report on their progress. How do you set your team up to monitor its own success?

1. **Every team meeting should be armed with data.** Your team must collect, analyze, and promote action plans with strong data. Be diligent about getting the facts and understanding them in the context of work before you judge their impact. Some teams collect tons of data, while others, especially those working in less tangible areas like training, strategy, or implementation teams, provide little or no data. Identify all the ways you can show that you have succeeded: people involved, messages delivered, feedback provided, steps proposed and completed, etc. For any project, there are some hard data and some soft data, and you should collect as much of both as possible. Ultimately you need to show value—how your team's work affects costs, profits, and productivity.

2. **Help every team advocate and sell its value.** Every employee and every team has to first understand and measure value, but then managers must help take data, new ideas, and recommendations for change to their superiors and to other teams to validate the work of their teams. Managers who ignore this role will find themselves fighting for people perceived as less important to the company or will struggle to keep people tuned in and excited about the work.

3. **Managers must be mentors.** Managers add value when they use their experience to help others learn, empowering them with the knowledge to be self-sufficient. Mentoring asks managers to bring their best knowledge and the best thinking they can find to their employees. And while managers are often the ones doing the mentoring, sometimes the best mentors are teammates or people from other teams. Remember that someone can be mentored by the same person he or she is mentoring on a different set of skills. Teams thrive when they create this kind of value sharing.

4. **Managers must be coaches.** Coaching is hard for many managers and is a skill that needs to be developed. It is an affirming process that helps employees feel valued and compelled to keep work moving forward. Many think of coaches as sports figures who yell and get in people's faces, but coaching in the modern workplace is a subtle, delicate technique in which the coach ensures that people are "caught doing things right," not just being chastised for mistakes.

5. **Managers must follow through and follow up.** The weakest link in management effectiveness is often follow-through and follow-up. This might be because managers, busy managers, have their own work and often have excellent excuses for not paying attention to the work of others. Follow-through is doing what you say you will do. Managers often promise help or increased budgets or to get senior management's support, or make a host of other promises that will help their teams succeed. Then they become the barrier when they don't follow through. In many cases the manager should have empowered the team member and connected that person directly with the people who could solve the problem; instead, the manager takes on the burden and then fails to follow through. Managers who are good at follow-through and empowerment find their teams to be more efficient, self-reliant, and productive than their counterparts who fail to follow through.

Follow-up is simply checking in and showing that you care. Teams will perform better if their work matters. Too often workers are given a task and receive no real contact for weeks or months. The upside is that if the employees are on track, they will have developed a sense of independence; the downside is that if they are off track, it may be too late to set things straight. Follow-up helps managers see and understand the work being done, and shows workers that they care that team members are doing what they committed to. Sometimes fake work happens in spite of good intentions, so managers must monitor and check up with employees to compare work against agreed-upon plans.

6. **Managers must ensure that others are accountable as well.** Managers are accountable to those above them, and therefore they must keep team members accountable for finishing critical tasks, aligning with priorities, meeting deadlines, and completing deliverables. This means that action plans or work plans must be broken down into specific actions that can be observed, quantified, and discussed with clarity. Each action needs a deadline and various milestones attached to it. When team members are prepared with this kind of information, they can be held accountable without question. Managers and team members should work together to create plans that will help them both understand and discuss the specifics of how the work is proceeding.

7. **Promote sharing.** Within your team and many of its related teams, great things will be happening. So set up simple and open methods to systematize new learning, best practices, and improved processes. Where there is new learning of value, share it. Where there are new tools, bring them into play for everyone. Where there are significant accomplishments, pass the word along.

In conclusion, managers are essential in narrowing the gap between fake work and real work. Managers can facilitate great work by ensuring that people are focused on the right work, connected to strategy, and have clear priorities. They can help teams align and work together in a unified way. They can help teams execute with excellence and drive the results the company is seeking. And, unfortunately, they can also be the very barriers to all those positive results. As gatekeepers, managers have a powerful opportunity to build trust and facilitate great work. If you are a manager, take those responsibilities seriously. People leave managers because too often the managers don't understand their responsibilities to their people and their company.

A Roadmap for Action

- Think about the ways your traditional approaches to management are an impediment to strong relationships, strong teams, and an open and honest workplace.

- List the skills, such as collaboration, empowerment, and modeling, that you need to work on to be a better manager and a better employee.

- Think about how you can better understand your company's strategies and the intent of those strategies.

- Consider how you can increase your communication skills to share strategies with employees and teammates.

- Think about how you can do a better job of translating strategies into tasks that employees can execute.

- Determine how you can better set up the conditions for alignment so that employees will share and help each other improve focus and work.

- Consider how you will change your approach to performance management so you can link it to alignment and work priorities with the whole team.

- Identify the barriers in the workplace that are particularly distracting to you and your team. How can you mitigate the negative effects on your work?

- Determine what practices you need to learn about or share, and how you will work with other teams, groups, or departments to learn more about successes that you can capitalize on.

PATH 9

Strive for a Real-Work Company Culture

I probably worked just as hard at AT&T as I do now.
It was just on the wrong things: the power struggles,
the budget debates, the political issues.

—Alex Mandl

PATH 9 IS about how a company's culture influences both fake and real work. It is, to some extent, a summation of the other paths as they converge. So, what is company culture? It is the sum of the people and personalities within the company and all the influences that have a bearing on the company. This includes customers, executive-level leaders, all other leaders, shareholders, and each employee who works each day in the company. Together, they all influence whether the company culture promotes fake work or fosters real work.

You and your company culture are important. And you, wherever you are in the company, influence the culture in a significant way.

This path is about the difficulties we face as members of our company culture. It explores how the culture we work in makes us more effective at some times and less effective at other times. And it helps to answer why some companies thrive, some fail, and some change for the better; why some do lots of fake work and lots of real work.

This path will explain the following steps for overcoming and re-creating your company culture to make it a more effective culture for doing real work.

Step 1: Develop a vision of what you want your company culture to be.

Step 2: Establish real work as a core cultural value.

Step 3: Assess real-work culture by looking at results.

Step 4: Promote systems, structures, and processes that support a culture of real work.

Step 5: Set up the conditions for cultural change.

Path 9 is important because company culture constitutes rules, customs, traditions, and norms that determine everything from when and where people eat their lunch to who will succeed, fail, gain power, or gain influence in an organization. Employees who work for a company while ignorant of its culture are like foreigners trying to drive cars in a distant land without any knowledge of the traffic laws there. And while the "rules" of a culture are usually unwritten, they are still enforced, and in the workplace one must learn them by asking questions and observing what behaviors are practiced by those who are rewarded or promoted, as well as by those who don't advance, are demoted, or are let go. The rules, expectations, and acceptable behaviors in a company are the outward manifestations of its culture.

Before we go any further, let's look at an example of the impact that company culture can have in the workplace—and how easy it can be to misinterpret that culture.

WHAT IS THE CULTURE OF SUPERIOR SERVICE?

A newly hired mechanic named Jim was told that superior service to the customer was the creed of the whole shop. Jim's supervisor emphasized that if he would just remember this one concept, Jim would do as well as any mechanic in the company.

Being well trained in auto mechanics, Jim worked hard to please his customers during his first morning on the job. In fact, by the time he was ready to take a break, he was exhausted. Jim was happy to see that there were no customers in sight, and taking his sack lunch and soda, Jim found a clean spot on the shop floor, sat down, and began to eat. He was glad to be off his feet, as his legs ached from standing all morning.

But as soon as Jim had seated himself comfortably on the shop floor, his supervisor startled him with a curse, yelling, "Get off your butt, Jim! I thought I told you there's never any sitting around here. Imagine what would happen if the regional store director stopped by and saw you plopped down there?"

Jim was shocked. Jumping up, he protested to his supervisor that he had worked harder than any other mechanic that morning, that his legs were tired, and that the shop had no chairs in it. Then his supervisor explained that it just didn't look right to have a uniformed mechanic sitting on the shop floor—even during lunch. Jim learned that he was supposed to go into a back room or outside to sit.

The unwritten rule about never sitting on the shop floor was an outward manifestation of the values and norms of the service center culture. Workers always had to appear to be actively in the service of the customer, that was a big part of the company culture. Jim learned about the culture in the service center the hard way. If another mechanic had just given him a few hints, Jim could have avoided this unpleasant experience on his first day at work.

Jim was not doing fake work, he was doing real work; but he was not yet aware of the influence the company culture had on his work. However, sometimes company culture can do more than just embarrass you—it can cause you to do fake work, as illustrated by the following story.

ON THE CUTTING EDGE

When I was transferred to a new product team, I couldn't have been more excited. I was picked after being recommended by several leaders. Claude, a new high-level executive, called me personally and asked me to be on his team. He was going to take our company into a whole new cutting-edge technology by leveraging the burgeoning smart-phone market. Our company created specialty products for heavy equipment; we had never been in this competitive space in the market. However, we could see where this gave us a boost with our very specialized suppliers and their relationships with us.

This was a big deal because it would launch a whole new group of products for the company. We weren't really a technology company, so the formation of this team signaled a whole new direction. All we had to do was create partnership agreements with current technology developers and we could create a whole new product line. The project was backed by large budgets of money and lots of top people.

The first chapter of this story is that we all went to work. We researched the products, services, demographics, resources, suppliers, etc. We put together an amazing array of information.

In the second chapter we put together PowerPoint presentations and position papers, and we met with the top brass. We sold an amazing concept, and it looked like solid gold.

In Chapter 3, several of us started asking about the big assumption Claude had considered as a given: Would our clients, our buyers, be looking for this kind of product, and more important, would they purchase this product from us?

We decided to start talking to our salespeople and our clients. They all thought we were—to put it bluntly—idiots. While we had a great reputation among our clients for our other services, it made no sense for them to buy this kind of product from us when the big players would always be ahead of us, cost less, and provide better packages. We looked like fools.

You would think that the whole process would have spun out of control at this point, but Claude is very charismatic. Claude's main goal was to keep executives on the hook with reasons to maintain his plans. In the meantime, the rest of us started scurrying to find a way out before the project imploded.

We learned later that Claude had been a big shot at another company and was pushed out for doing the same thing he'd done at my company—creating a whole new world out of papier-mâché. He had convinced our low-tech, naive leadership of his genius and sold them on ideas that may have had value to others in the tech field, but that were totally irrelevant for our company. I hate to admit how many people were taking their eye off the ball and how many of us were willing to jump on board with this crazy idea. But Claude is a whirlwind. He can make you change your beliefs. Unfortunately he can't produce.

The company culture allowed Claude to do what he did. People were punished by their lack of insight into the company's competencies. Every company, as part of its culture, must know its core products and core competencies. That is how wild plans are avoided. Fake work ensued because people were willing to ignore the clues, even as company leaders were ignoring core processes, core products, and core services— and being manipulated by schemes.

What to Know About Path 9

Company Cultures Evolve, and Each Is Different

Company culture initially grows out of the behaviors of those who established them, and then by all those who follow. The culture takes on the personalities of key founders, dominant players, and charismatic leaders—clearly, the culture at Google or Starbucks is drastically different than at Citibank or Honda. Company culture exists regardless of attempts to ignore it. A company culture builds over time, with many different factors influencing it. A few key factors that affect a company's culture are:

- **People.** The people a company recruits and hires greatly influence the company's culture.
- **Company policies.** Policies such as vacation days, overtime, dispute resolution, cell phone use, etc.

- **Company values.** Values such as how to deal with people and how to handle clients have much to do with the company culture.
- **The industry.** Companies in the same industry often take on a similar culture. The culture is quite different in the automobile manufacturing industry than in the computer industry.
- **Company leadership.** Leaders influence the culture immensely. Differing personalities and leadership styles have a great impact on company culture.
- **Mergers and acquisitions.** When companies go through huge changes like mergers or acquisitions, their company cultures are greatly influenced.

These and other factors blend to create the composite company culture. And that culture has a strong impact on both real and fake work.

Company Culture Is a Leading Driver of Fake Work

The following story comes from a colleague, a strategy and organizational development consultant, who had been on a series of projects in the health care industry. It is a perfect example of how a culture can poison an otherwise successful company.

CREATING A LABYRINTH WITH NO WAY OUT

As part of my consulting group's team, I was assigned to a large project initiated by a Fortune 500 company. This company was at the top of its game in their industry and had, over the course of several years, acquired close to a hundred other companies. The parent company maintained and promoted a carefully articulated, well-focused strategic plan for all its subsidiaries, which included allowing these companies to continue functioning, in large measure, as independent entities.

Among its strategies was an initiative to streamline processes throughout the company and to create synergies among the various subsidiaries. Out of that grew a specific focus on contracting, with the goal of reducing overhead, eliminating redundancies, and—most important—stopping the loss of customers who were often confused by the differences in contracts, billing procedures, return policies, and the like that came from what they perceived as the same corporation.

The executive team's analysts as well as the first wave of its consultants (which included my group) estimated that this initiative could save the company at least $700 million in internal costs over three to five years, not to mention hanging on to millions in revenues that might otherwise be lost.

A very knowledgeable and experienced senior executive named Madison was assigned to direct a steering committee for this initiative. In addition to firmly grasping the processes, she was great at navigating the company culture, working the system, and building relationships with key individuals. She also saw the minefields, which included the presidents of the various subsidiaries, who didn't much care for any interference with their individual empires.

Madison quickly rehired our consulting group (which had worked with the executive team in developing this initiative) to help assess the problems, as well as three other consulting groups to map the processes, to analyze content, and to create a detailed project plan to integrate key people from all of the companies.

Among other inefficiencies, our team found that the hours involved in executing and implementing the various companies' contracts were out of control. The overall process had roughly two hundred steps, each of which was done manually. This led to an error rate of over 75 percent, with each error leading to a complete manual review of all the documents. Madison soon turned her attention toward implementing a unified and automated IT system that would standardize and simplify all the documents, invoices, reports, etc., associated with the company's contracts. Then, as we began looking at a change process to get all the players from all the subsidiaries scattered all across the country on board, the project hit a brick wall.

Despite our efforts to bring the various company presidents together to solve problems, the presidents would not act. The cause, which was deeply imbedded in the culture, was simple: Each of the individual companies had lots of autonomy. They were also successful. And the mind-set of their presidents was, almost universally, "I will run my company as I see fit!"

In an effort to overcome this obstacle, Madison hired our consulting company once again, and she had us analyze all the data that had been collected up to then, and to interview key people in each of the companies. Then she had our consultants prepare several presentations for the corporate executive team, detailing the scope of the problem we were trying to resolve, which by now had nearly doubled—to $1.4 billion. With each presentation, she sought support from the executive team. In addition to outlining the much-needed changes in processes, she detailed the lack of cooperation from the division presidents and the cost of the slowdown. Each time she was told to rethink her strategy.

So she made adjustments, brought in new people, changed the methodology, met with the presidents, and extracted promises. But, after each cycle, she found that the presidents wouldn't let their people attend meetings, be trained, make changes, or participate in implementation teams. Finally, after two years and lots of stagnation, she was dismissed from the project and most of her team was disbanded, including our consulting group.

John, another executive, took over Madison's role, and he lasted about eighteen months. Ramsey, a third executive, took over for him, and at the end of his first year, our team was brought back on board for the third time—four and a half years after Madison had undertaken the initiative. This is where I got involved. My first task was to research the history of the project and determine our current status and how the project had gotten to this point. That work was extensive.

Then I was assigned to system design, while other team members were assigned to mapping processes. What we quickly learned, though, was that we were mostly copying systems and processes from older documents. All of this had been done before! It was as though we had each been cast for the lead role in *Groundhog Day*.

But we were a determined bunch, and we began making recommendations and developing plans for implementation. Our first recommendation was that the executive team put some teeth behind its directives to the presidents. That was not done. We then developed a series of training meetings designed to bring small groups from the various subsidiaries together. Out of the first round of twelve that were scheduled, all but two had to be canceled for lack of participation.

After being turned down cold by president after president, we tried to tell Ramsey that, if we couldn't make some progress, he would be fired. His response, verbatim, was: "As long as I can show that work is being done, I'll be okay."

Beyond the internal costs, the company spent close to $30 million on consultants, yet our work provided no concrete changes. And while the company had been at the top of its industry when the initiative was started, currently the company is under fire, its stock is down, shareholders are concerned about inefficiencies, and competitors are breaking into areas where this company once dominated.

And, yes, Ramsey got fired.

The previous story illustrates the complex web of fake work that can breed within a company culture. It shows how the very rules of the established culture can encourage fake work. In this case, the cultural norms allowed all the acquired companies to do business in their own unique ways. In companies where you hear people say, "And this too shall pass," the way that Ramsey did, they are admitting to a company culture that likes to launch ships—new ideas, initiatives, and change—but doesn't really like to implement change. Employees soon assume that they don't really need to do anything—they just have to wait for the ship to sink.

Dozens of key decision makers and ultimately hundreds of people at this company propagated an environment of fake work. What fake-work factors were at work in this culture? The following is a short list of the many lessons from this story:

- **Fake work had infiltrated the culture.** The company had set up a variety of patterns that allowed, supported, and even rewarded fake work. People were being paid, promoted, and validated for outcomes that were failures. Further, they set up a pattern where mavericks ruled.
- **The leadership allowed fake work by failing to set expectations and measure results.** A group of highly paid, intelligent leaders simply ignored their own initiative, their investments, and their agreement with directors to push the initiative through.
- **The CEO could have turned this around quickly, but didn't.** The entire initiative should have been dropped because it wasn't a priority, or it should have been boosted to a higher priority to get it done.
- **The presidents of the various divisions sabotaged the new initiative.** They either flagrantly pushed against it or just waited for it to fail. They were barriers, very costly barriers, to any progress, and they weren't honest with the executive team.
- **Managers in the targeted areas were not supportive.** Everyone knew the system was broken. The managers could have benefited by partnering with the project team, pushing against the operational leaders, and changing broken processes.
- **The project directors chose fake work over results.** These directors were high performers who were being tasked with critical work. Sadly, these executives literally changed their

performance measures from success to any activity at all—promoting fake work.

- **Consultants and the consulting company's leadership failed to take a stand.** These professionals learned, very quickly, that they were being paid to pave a road to nowhere. However, to them, doing work, even fake work—and billing for it—justified their roles. Clearly, their customers' best interests and their own personal integrity were negotiable.

- **Workers in the divisions, working under managers who reported to the presidents, knew systems needed changing and ignored the problem.** Fake work never feels good, but hundreds of people were doing work that was ineffective, redundant, and unnecessary. The changes would have benefited everyone, but people at all levels all accepted a culture of fake work.

This is a sad story, and it is easy to see how the problems could have been fixed. Even sadder is the fact that this story is being played out again and again in many different companies in every industry, in nonprofits, in federal and state agencies, and in schools and community groups. And the underlying problem is the company culture.

It seems way too simple to suggest that someone just needs to start asking: "Are we doing fake work here?" But that may well be the first step to breaking up a fake-work culture.

Causes of Fake-Work Cultures

Many factors help create fake-work cultures. Many corporate processes, like decision making, change management, communication, and operations, are rife with fake work. But leadership and management are the standard-bearers for fake-work cultures. Below are some common characteristics of fake-work cultures:

1. **Autocratic leaders.** Autocratic leaders have launched entire ships of fake work by pursuing a product or an initiative that

many know is heading totally in the wrong direction. Millions of dollars' worth of fake work can happen with a single directive.

2. **Cavalier leaders.** In many companies, leaders fail to establish the environment for success and to aid alignment and execution. When they don't take those roles seriously, they enable the wrong behaviors.

3. **Unclear business and strategic plans.** Writing and communicating strategic plans is worthless if employees remain clueless about strategic direction. One company told us that it had invested heavily in linking its people to its plans. But our research showed that over 70 percent of the employees there had no real understanding of the strategies.

4. **A lack of clear company values.** Values are the navigational stars in a company. If managers do not articulate them, model and live them, monitor and set expectations to follow them, people will do work that fails the best intentions of the company. Articulating a value like "safety" can mean the difference between success and failure in an organization.

5. **Being removed from the customer.** Cultures that don't stay close to customer needs create fake work by guessing incorrectly about those needs. Companies also need to help focus staff functions, HR, legal support, and IT because they are notorious fake-work spawning sites where lots of gaps open up between programs and real work.

6. **Short-sighted thinking.** Business often suffers from having only one strategy—maximizing profits. Every other strategy becomes a victim to short-term profits. Sometimes companies cut costs in areas like customer service for short-term gains. A ton of people then end up shifting their work to deal with customer complaints, lagging sales, and angry stockholders.

7. **Arrogance and complacency.** Some companies can't imagine that the competition will ever catch up. Those companies are

monuments to fake work because they don't listen to their employees, their customers, and the trends in the marketplace.

8. **A constant influx of new systems, structures, and procedures.** Companies too often work on new systems that cause tons of work to get them up, running, and implemented. In an effort to improve effectiveness, companies target process change without ensuring that they are linked to the business goals they are addressing.

9. **Old-school performance management processes.** In most companies, the way they manage, review, and reward performance is totally ineffective. These processes don't help manage performance at all.

10. **Failure to train and build managers.** The investment in managers and the insistence on managers of high quality and high value are minimal in too many companies.

11. **A tendency to hire people without clear expectations tied to competencies and company goals.** People are hired all the time to fill a position rather than to focus on a problem or to bring a set of competencies to a role.

12. **Fast growth without controls.** Some companies have created cultures that are often exciting to work in because everything seems like real work, critical work, and people are passionate about it. However, fake work isn't just what you are doing, sometimes it is what you are not doing. Over time, much of your work can become fake.

These factors that affect company culture will ultimately alter the culture that you may be pursuing or hoping for. In the following sections we will provide ways to reduce fake work caused by a flawed company culture.

Steps to Move Down Path 9

Companies are only as strong as the sum of their employees' individual strengths. Therefore, each of us has a role to play in the development and the perception of our company's culture. The following steps focus primarily on companies and their leaders, but it's important to also remember that people throughout the company are the real measure of the strength of the culture.

Step 1: Develop a Vision of What You Want Your Company Culture to Be

Ultimately, do you really know what the culture of your company is? Do you know what you want your culture to be? Do you know how you want to be perceived by your customers, your employees, or your shareholders? Companies spend lots of time on the mission and the goals of the business, but often they just let the company culture develop. Companies often fail to realize the impact their culture has on real work and spend too little time considering the effects their choices have on their culture. For instance, we hear company leaders talk about how they want their organization to be considered customer-oriented. What does it take to get there? If you want your company to be focused on customer service, make sure that the messages, systems, and processes you put in place reflect that, or you will get a different culture by default. Some organizations with a service goal actually reward cost cutting that detracts from customer service groups, time with the customer, and initiatives to better serve the customer.

Look at the strategies you've developed, consider the messages you are sending, and focus on your vision. Creating a vision and seeing it come to fruition takes foresight, diligence, and commitment. Consider how people, processes, and rewards reflect your vision, and then establish the behaviors and values that will best reflect and facilitate that vision. Finally, open up your culture to get honest feedback about variances in the workplace that work against the culture. Shifts in culture are challenging for many people, so implementing them takes time, understanding, and encouragement.

Step 2: Establish Real Work as a Core Cultural Value

As important as mission, vision, objectives, and strategies are, a culture is built on values. Many of us have worked with companies that have blatant disregard for the values they espouse, or don't espouse any values at all. Whatever the case, the company culture is determined by what is done, not by what is said, and values provide focal points that help us evaluate our choices for how we treat each other, how we engage with each other, and how we value the company and its customers.

The first value a company holds should be the commitment to doing real work. To get real and valued results, real work must be an overriding and constant value. If you buy into the premise and all the steps we've suggested to build a real-work culture, you have to set expectations for real work and you must do the following:

- You must have employees who ask about fake work and ask for clarity and definition.
- You must support employees who say no to fake work.
- You must stop rewarding people who do fake work.

In addition, your company's values should be written and be behaviorally based. The behaviors must be observed and promoted in good faith. The values shouldn't just be platitudes and ideals, although they should be idealistic. Avoid writing simple value statements like "We believe in being honest, fair, and resourceful." These statements are devoid of meaning and clarity. Instead, take key words or ideas and state them in a way that helps people apply them, as in the following examples:

VALUE STATEMENTS

Value Goal	Value Description
Financial Success	• Be accountable for managing costs, improving profits, and managing the business to support the needs of all stakeholders balanced with the long-term needs of the business and its people.
Balance	• Promote a work style that incorporates hard work, fun, and time for personal renewal.
Diversity	• Promote diversity in every aspect of our business: hiring, developing, and promoting. Promote diversity with our customers and in our approach to all of our work.
Sustainability	• Direct projects and manage the business in a manner that conserves resources and demonstrates respect for the environments in which we live and work.

These are examples of actual value statements from companies we have worked with. They differ from company to company, but some should always be based on the business, some on the people, and some on the community in which we live. The statements can easily get long and overwhelming when considering many differing inputs, but they can usually be edited and combined into a manageable, accessible list.

Whatever your values, they should be stated with a sense of financial reality and with an understanding of the most important elements of the business.

Step 3: Assess Your Real-Work Culture by Looking at Results

If real work is a core value—and it must be if you want your company to be successful—then you cannot accept fake work. To that end, you must constantly assess your work and your culture through the lens of the work itself.

To do that effectively, attach measures of success to every strategy and every critical task that is quantifiable or observable, and discuss performance based on those measures. Employees will often struggle with these new measures, but they will soon learn that data helps them build their case for their value, rather than being subject to a supervisor's guessing and tainted memories. The two simple examples in the table on pages 214-15 show how to make measures more useful even with tasks that seem hard to measure.

Think of success as being connected to the real-work culture you want and need. What defines your success? Are you willing to ask the tough questions about why people or customers are leaving your company? When you are shaping the company culture, are you defining success by results? Google, for example, has game rooms and plenty of ways for employees to seemingly get diverted. But the company measures by results, not activity. Real work is productive. Real work is centered. Real work isn't just being busy and keeping things in motion. In the modern workplace, knowledge and ideas are hard to measure, but they should be focused and measured by results.

Focus on the customer. What results do your customers want and need? The customer isn't always right, but the customer's beliefs are almost always important. What customers want or think they want are what shapes the marketplace you are trying to survive in.

Think long term. While many short-term issues dominate our days, all of us—in all aspects of our lives—need to think about the results or outcomes we are seeking.

Be purposeful. Without clear purpose, without clear plans, we

Critical Task	Weak Measure	Better Measure	Best Measure
Implement the sales of the new services package.	Check to see that all salespeople are introducing the new service package.	Request reporting on all clients where the new service package has been introduced, along with customer feedback.	• Demand reports from all salespeople on introductions of the new package. • Collect client responses to the new package from all salespeople. • Join salespeople on calls to check effectiveness of the new message. • Check and ensure that at least 35% of sales are linked to the new service package. • Follow up with customers on their perception of the value of the package.

Critical Task	Weak Measure	Better Measure	Best Measure
Train all employees in Accounting on the new XYZ software.	Get all the employees trained.	Get all the employees trained and ensure they understand the content and the changes.	• Establish a current baseline for speed and error rates on the current software. • Train 100% of the employees. • Test for at least 80% knowledge of new content. • Validate that 100% are applying it on the job. • Check against the baseline to show improvements and increased productivity.

are likely to find ourselves doing fake work. Engage in every element of your day with purpose and clear intent.

Clearly state the results you are seeking at every opportunity (or ask for them to be stated). For example:

- At a meeting: "The purpose of this meeting is to determine the problems we are facing with the implementation of this process and how to fix them."
- On a call: "Hi, Rosa, thanks for finding time for me. I'm calling to make sure I understand the details of your order and how to get it to you immediately."
- When starting a project: "The purpose of this project is to redesign the processes for testing and review. We want to address the areas of concern, but ultimately we want to make the system better by streamlining it and cutting costs, redundancies, and useless reporting processes."
- When helping a coworker: "My understanding is that you are struggling with the financial conversions for the billing for England. If so, then I would like to show you the method for doing this one and the ones you will deal with in the future."

Step 4: Promote Systems, Structures, and Processes That Support a Culture of Real Work

If real work is a core value, you cannot tolerate antiquated systems, inefficient processes, and dilapidated structures that work against the results you are seeking. To weed out potential problems, ask the questions that will best address real work. For example:

- Do our financial structure and financial systems support the values of our company and work in the best interests of our employees?
- Do our policies constrain elements in the culture that need to be more open and responsive?

- Do procedures and protocols make us less flexible and adaptable?
- Are hiring policies supporting the culture and the values of the company?
- Are decisions made with real work in mind or in the interests of those making the decisions?
- Are communication processes failing to give employees the quality information they need? Or is communication working at odds with the best interests of employees by overwhelming or confusing them?
- Are the tools we need to succeed helpful or hindering our success?

The goal is to promote real work and disavow yourself of work that is not bringing value.

Step 5: Set Up the Conditions for Cultural Change

If real work is your core value, then stagnation works against all your best interests. Company culture is an organic, dynamic mix of complex and changing elements. It seldom stands still, because while company cultures can stay similar in style, they often have to change in substance and approach to reflect a constantly changing marketplace and constantly shifting workforce.

Cultural change is not an event. It is a process. It takes time, involvement, buy-in, commitment, and follow-through that can seem interminable and exhausting when you're in the middle of it. And yet companies that are prepared for and foster cultural change are less likely to have serious interruptions to the flow of work during the cycles of change.

Some companies avoid change, which is very hard and counterproductive. And when change comes, they avoid communicating, collaborating, and involving the many people who will need to both go through the change and manage the stability of the work in the company at the same time. Companies need to drive a culture where cultural change is continually evolving, and is not seen as a terrifying interruption. Sometimes when a company is going through adjustments in its culture (because of a merger, a system implementation, or a process change), the biggest impediment to change is the people. To build a responsive change culture, take the following measures:

- Write a communication strategy that focuses on culture change. Determine what you need to change, determine how you will communicate it, and communicate it often over time, through various media.
- Write value statements about culture change. In addition to the values outlined above, consider including values about change as an inherent expectation in your company.
- Promote the benefits of a culture change. People are willing to change if they know what is in it for them and the company—both of which are important to their own security.
- Be selective about culture change. When a company is involved in too many initiatives, culture change may feel like chaos.
- Be precise.
- Get everyone involved.
- Promote alignment, collaboration, relationship-building, and teamwork to build support systems for people and create momentum.
- Empower people to solve problems and promote trust.

A real-work culture is a highly interdependent network of people working together to serve the company strategy. The better your company defines its mission and objectives, articulates strategies, aligns people, and executes work, the more likely it is that the company will evolve into a high-performance culture where everyone is working toward the same goal—absolute success.

A Roadmap for Action

- Consider the meaning of culture and how it can affect real or fake work.

- Create a vision of the culture you want and need to succeed.

- Assess your culture to see how close you are to your vision.

- Plan how to fill the gap between your vision and reality.

- Write out and communicate the values that reflect the vision of the culture. Make sure one of those values is to "promote real work."

- Set up the systems for collecting data, measuring success, and managing people to ensure they are all focused on results.

- Look at your systems, structures, and processes—along with policies and procedures—to ensure they support your culture of real work.

- Set up a plan for cultural change, and work to set up the conditions of change so that employees are partners in the process and not victims of it.

- Work!

EPILOGUE
Choose the Road to Real Work

I shall be telling this with a sigh
Somewhere ages and ages hence:
Two roads diverged in a wood, and I—
I took the one less traveled by,
And that has made all the difference.

— Robert Frost

FAKE WORK IS a massive problem. It exists everywhere and keeps people in organizations from doing the work that needs to be done, the real work that would lead to organizational results. So what can you do about it?

You can *choose* to do what's right for your company; you can choose to do real work! Only you can make a difference. Whatever your level, you are personally faced with eliminating as much fake work as possible in your company and in every other organization you belong to. Ultimately, the benefits are yours as well—because real work is endlessly more rewarding than fake work.

In the preceding chapters we have provided you with definitions, causes of fake work, and paths to lead you away from fake work. So now what? You must make a choice and you must *act* on your choice. But you can't be cavalier about it; fake work is like a disease that has spread to the organs and tissues of the whole organization, and you don't just fix it—you diagnose it, you work on it, and you keep fighting it over time.

How do you take action? You have to attack major problems by focusing on work—on getting people to do real work. You can and must attack the simple and obvious problems of fake work by addressing those things under your control. These things are addressed in every chapter. Make a list. Attack. Then reap the benefits of real work.

If fake work were as simple as it seems, we wouldn't have written the book. (The exercise itself would've been fake work!) But fake work is a complicated issue that requires integrated work across teams and across the company to really conquer serious problems. The big idea of this book is *not* about what is easy to see, but about the subversive and eroding aspects of organizational processes that end up creating massive amounts of fake work. It requires time, attention, and creative processes to change teams, cultures, and finally the company's bottom line. Think about how you implement—top to bottom—and find the gaps in that chain. Start filling them in—do real work.

The Robert Frost poem "The Road Not Taken" was not written with fake work in mind, but it was written about making choices. We believe the road less traveled is the road to real work. We challenge you to take the road less traveled, even though the decision could be difficult. Choose the road to real work and to a more productive world. Now, make your choice and take action and start building a road to somewhere—act to eliminate as much fake work as you can!

Remember that a fake-work road leads to nowhere! Get to real work!

ACKNOWLEDGMENTS

WE ARE DEEPLY indebted to many who have helped us make this book possible. We have been blessed by their friendship, contributions, and suggestions. Together, we would like to acknowledge a few of these wonderful people.

Jim Bell for his commitment to this book and for being a confidant, friend, golfing partner, reader, and reviewer, and most of all for being an anchor in the winds.

Julie Reiser and Tom Lovell, who helped us work through and shape early drafts. They helped us find our center and kept us pounding at the issues until we could begin to articulate them. We especially appreciated their hard work, friendship, and humor.

Stephen M. R. Covey and Greg Link, who have worked with us to make this book a reality. Their experience has helped lead the way. They are friends and colleagues of the highest order.

Emily Westlake, because she is everything you could hope for in an editor—someone who understands and works to maintain the integrity of the content while making our writing accessible.

Michael Broussard for his excitement about the content and for helping make the book a reality.

Håkan Palm for his contribution to the ideas and early focus on the problems that helped define fake work.

Stephen Krempl, a longtime friend and advocate, for helping facilitate our work and our ideas.

Darryl Wee, Pam Britton, and Mary Fox, who have been advocates for doing real work and doing it well.

Many friends, clients, and colleagues who have shared their fake-work stories with us. Many, many clients who have dedicated time and energy to getting work right and testing the content, and for helping discriminate fake from real work.

In addition, Brent would like to thank:

My wife Arlene for her spiritual support, her great critiques, and her friendship and love for the last forty-two years. Thanks to my children Amy and her husband David Hirtle, Dan and his wife Cathy, and Caroline and her husband Jon Blackham for their constant love, support, encouragement, and the best bunch of grandchildren a grandpa has ever had.

Stan Sinclair for his hard work with *The Work Itself* and for applying it. Craig Swenson for constant encouragement and belief in my work. Mike Gillespie for providing assistance and help at all times. Bee Wan Ditzig for her continued faith and trust in me and this book. Roger Dean Duncan and Curt Howes for being truly professional partners in every way.

And Gaylan would like to extend special thanks to:

Brent D. Peterson, my coauthor and business partner, because I learn something every day from him and because he is a dream friend and partner—insightful, practical, kind, caring, supportive, and many other adjectives.

To Elaine, my wife, a very special thanks for being a dedicated reviewer, a critical advocate for readers, and a better friend than I could possibly deserve. Thanks to my children: Harte Nielson, my son, has contributed immensely to the content of this book because he has been living it; my daughter Quisha and her husband, Steven Wilkinson; Harte's wife, Stephanie; and Hadley and her husband, Tyler Johnson, who have all played roles as readers, critics, passionate contributors, and reality watchdogs. I thank Hannah and Sasha, my granddaughters, who have filled my life with the humor, perspective, and joy I've needed to make this endeavor worth it. Thanks to my parents, Scott and Lila Nielson, for teaching me the joys of doing work of value, and for their sacrifices so I could have the joys and abundance life has brought my way. Scott Jr., Mark, and Wendy, my siblings, have made survival and success possible.

My thanks to a few special friends as well: David Kranes, for being a creative mentor and friend for so long that I will always be spiritually linked to him and his influence; Tom Goldsmith and Mary Tull, who are friends, gurus, and leaders in my life, and great advocates for this book; Mary Whitesides, everything a sister-in-law could possibly be—a friend, a colleague, and an adventurer and guide, who paved a path to the rest of the world; and Peter Seyderhelm for being a business ally, and to him and his wife, Amanda, for their immense friendship.

INDEX

ABOUT THE AUTHORS

BRENT D. PETERSON is cofounder and chair of the Work Itself Group. He is a keynote speaker, author, and adviser on strategy, alignment, and execution, as well as an advocate for education and training that makes a difference to people and organizations, who consults with companies and addresses audiences around the world. Brent has been a professor in the Marriott School of Management at Brigham Young University, has written twenty books, and has been an owner/founder of three consulting companies. He resides with his wife, Arlene, in the Rocky Mountains.

GAYLAN W. NIELSON is cofounder and CEO of the Work Itself Group. He is dedicated to linking strategy to alignment and execution, and consults, speaks, and writes about those processes all the time. He has been a consultant for more than twenty-two years, working around the United States and much of the world with clients at every level and every part of their organizations in a wide array of services. In another life, he wrote several plays (*RFD* was chosen for the Sundance Playwriting Conference), as well as radio plays with David Kranes (the series won an award and one of them won a Smithsonian prize), and he has published poetry, stories, and many articles. He is passionate about photography. He lives with Elaine, his wife, near Brent, in the Rocky Mountains.

LET US HELP YOU WITH FAKE WORK

We have antidotes for *Fake Work*. *Fake Work* grew out of our years of frustration working in the business and government workplace—the Road to Nowhere. *Fake Work* is about hard work that is often fake and the constant interference fake work causes to organizational results. But, just as the Paths in this book explore the journey to real work, our process, **The Work Itself,** is designed to address those issues and to solve them. **The Work Itself Group**, led by the authors, has focused our efforts to develop a package of services to help you identify, troubleshoot, and solve fake work with different approaches customized to client needs. A sample of our key services follows:

Fake Work Workshop – This one-day workshop is a focused look at fake work in the workplace and in your lives. We dive down into the concepts and help you understand and address fake work practically and interactively.

The Work Itself Process – The Work Itself Process drives strategies to the work employees do every day. It helps organizations align employees to their strategies so they can execute them and get results. The centerpiece of the process is a facilitated work session that encourages the individual employee, through the lens of their team, to align their individual and team activities with organizational strategy. **The Work Itself Process** encourages every employee to execute strategy by eliminating **fake work** and focusing on **real work**. Many organizations have benefited from applying **The Work Itself Process** to their efforts to execute effectively.

Assessments, Tools, Workshops, and Follow-up Processes – This is a comprehensive set of services to partner with clients to discover more about where fake work is unraveling strategic intentions. It also includes training and learning efforts with leaders, managers, and workers at all levels.

Most organizations have built strategic plans. However, not many organizations have been able to implement their strategy throughout their organization. Often organizations are struggling to get everyone to buy into and act on the strategic plan so the strategy works.

THE WORK ITSELF GROUP

ABOUT
THE WORK ITSELF GROUP

THE VALUE OF THE WORK ITSELF PROCESS

The Work Itself Process was developed as a result of The Work Itself Group's experience in strategic planning, quality improvement, and performance management.

A work team is the place where strategy is successfully implemented. When each individual in each work team in an organization is focused on strategy, everyone benefits.

STRATEGY → ALIGNMENT → EXECUTION

The Work Itself Process brings the whole organization together to create common focus. No single individual or group has the wisdom or ability to chart strategic action and carry it out successfully. To ensure that plans are sound, accepted, supported, and acted on, all human resources available to an organization must contribute to the process. The process was designed to get measurable results and a significant return on investment.

The Work Itself Work Session can be completed in one to two days, depending on the size of the work team. We will help you assess strategy, build plans, and set up follow-up sessions that create a laser focus on the actual work that needs to be done. We provide a simple, practical approach to accomplishing this ambitious goal.

CONTACT US FOR MORE INFORMATION AT:

The Work Itself Group
1-866-909-WORK
theworkitselfgroup.com

Contact the authors directly at:
brent@theworkitselfgroup.com
gaylan@theworkitself.com